UNDERSTANDING TREASURY BILLS AND OTHER U.S. GOVERNMENT SECURITIES

Read this No Nonsense Guide if you want to know about:

* ★ the world's most popular investment
* ★ how the United States deficit can work for you
* ★ the safest investment money can buy . . . backed by the security and strength of the United States government.
* ★ high yielding, flexible, liquid investments
* ★ Ginnie Maes and zero-coupon bonds
* ★ the pluses and minuses of owning U.S. Savings Bonds

D1215263

THE NO NONSENSE LIBRARY

NO NONSENSE FINANCIAL GUIDES

How to Finance Your Child's College Education, Revised Edition
How to Use Credit and Credit Cards, Revised Edition
Understanding Tax-Exempt Bonds
Understanding Money Market Funds, Revised Edition
Understanding Mutual Funds, Revised Edition
Understanding IRA's, Revised Edition
Understanding Treasury Bills and Other U.S. Government Securities, Revised Edition
Understanding Common Stocks, Revised Edition
Understanding the Stock Market, Revised Edition
Understanding Stock Options and Futures Markets
How to Choose a Discount Stockbroker, Revised Edition
How to Make Personal Financial Planning Work for You
How to Plan and Invest for Your Retirement
The New Tax Law and What It Means to You

NO NONSENSE REAL ESTATE GUIDES

Understanding Condominiums and Co-ops, Revised Edition
Understanding Buying and Selling a House, Revised Edition
Understanding Mortgages and Home Equity Loans, Revised Edition
Refinancing Your Mortgage, Revised Edition

NO NONSENSE LEGAL GUIDES

Understanding Estate Planning and Wills, Revised Edition
How to Choose a Lawyer

NO NONSENSE CAREER GUIDES

How to Use Your Time Wisely
Managing People—At Home, At Work
No Nonsense Interviewing

NO NONSENSE SUCCESS GUIDES

NO NONSENSE STUDY GUIDES

NO NONSENSE HEALTH GUIDES

NO NONSENSE COOKING GUIDES

NO NONSENSE PARENTING GUIDES

NO NONSENSE WINE GUIDES

NO NONSENSE CAR GUIDES

NO NONSENSE FINANCIAL GUIDE®

UNDERSTANDING TREASURY BILLS AND OTHER U.S. GOVERNMENT SECURITIES

Revised Edition

Arnold Corrigan
& Phyllis C. Kaufman

LONGMEADOW PRESS

To Steven L. Osterweis, with affection and gratitude

Understanding Treasury Bills and Other U.S. Government Securities, Revised Edition

Copyright © 1985, 1987 by Arnold Corrigan and Phyllis C. Kaufman. All rights reserved.

Cover art by November and Lawrence.
Production services by William S. Konecky Associates, New York.

Published by Longmeadow Press, 201 High Ridge Road, Stamford, Connecticut 06904. No part of this book may be reproduced or used in any form or by any means, electronic or mechanical, including photocopying, recording, or by any information storage and retrieval system, without permission in writing from the publisher.

No Nonsense Financial Guide is a trademark controlled by Longmeadow Press.

ISBN: 0-681-40242-3

Printed in the United States of America
0 9 8 7 6 5 4 3 2

CONTENTS

CONTENTS

PART I
LENDING TO UNCLE SAM

1 · THE WORLD'S FAVORITE INVESTMENT

INVESTORS ALL OVER THE world buy United States government securities.

U.S. Treasury bills, notes and bonds are, in a very real sense, the world's favorite investment.

Safety

Why? There are several reasons, but certainly the prime reason is *safety*. Most Americans accept the idea that the securities of the U.S. government are the safest investment they can buy. But this isn't simply the loyalty of U.S. citizens to their own government. Investors all over the world feel the same way. Money for investment pours into the U.S. from every corner of the globe, and a good portion of this inflow goes into the securities of the U.S. government.

This deserves a moment's thought. Americans take the stability of their government, and the safety of government securities, largely for granted. In most countries, people can't make those assumptions. While *we* may have doubts about our own economy, *they* generally view the U.S. as still the strongest, richest, most secure country in the world. And if they can, they put part of their money here for safety.

You don't have to understand world economics in order to invest intelligently in U.S. Treasury bills, bonds and other securities. But it's important to appreciate the very special qualities of these securities, which can hardly be duplicated elsewhere.

Liquidity

While *safety* is probably the first quality everyone thinks of with respect to government securities, another of their great advantages is *liquidity*. An investment is *liquid* when it can be easily turned into cash. Usually this depends on there being an active *market*, that is, a place to buy and sell the investment. The markets for U.S. government securities are the broadest in the world, with many billions of dollars' worth of securities traded every day. If you should happen to be the fortunate owner, say, of $100 million in Treasury bills, notes or bonds, you can easily sell them on any business day with relatively little effect on the market. You would receive your cash a day later. No strain, no problem. For both big and small investors, the liquidity advantage applies.

2· HOW YOU CAN PROFIT FROM THE U.S. DEFICIT

EVERYONE KNOWS THAT THE budget deficit of the U.S. government is a terrible thing. It causes (or helps cause) inflation, high interest rates, and a host of other problems.

We certainly don't quarrel with that point of view. But if you are an investor, the deficit may have some favorable side effects for you.

In recent years the federal budget deficit has risen to unprecedented levels of as high as *$200 billion* per year. That's the margin by which taxes have failed to cover expenses. To bridge this gap, the government has to *borrow* from individuals and large institutions such as banks, insurance companies, mutual funds, etc. As of the end of 1986, the total government debt had grown to well over *$2 trillion* ($2,000 billion).

High Interest Rates

If this is bad for the nation, in what way has it been good for investors, or at least certain types of investors? Very simply, the deficit has caused interest rates to be much higher than they otherwise would have been. In order to borrow hundreds of billions of dollars success-fully, the Treasury has had to pay much higher rates than in the past—at the peak in 1981–82, interest rates on long-term Treasury bonds averaged well over 13%, compared with rates of around 4% in the early 1960s. Since the rates paid on government securities are the cornerstone of the nation's interest rate structure, this has pushed up rates in every part of the economy.

No one knows precisely to what extent high inter-est rates are due to the federal budget deficit. But the deficit is certainly a major reason, and quite possibly *the* major reason.

Now You Can Have It All

From your standpoint as an investor, this change adds a great new attraction to government securities. Twenty-five years ago, investors assumed that if they chose the safety and liquidity of government securities, they had to accept a relatively low interest rate (yield). But in recent years, the yields have ranged from generous to remarkably high. In a sense, you can have your cake and eat it too.

3·JUST WHAT ARE U.S. GOVERNMENT SECURITIES?

BEFORE GOING FURTHER, we'd better define some of our terms. We've talked about government borrowing, and we've talked about investors buying U.S. government securities. These are all *debt* securities. For those who are not familiar with debt securities, a word of explanation may be helpful.

Debt Securities

In order to borrow effectively on a vast scale, the Treasury uses the mechanism of offering (that is, selling) debt securities to the public—to banks, other institutions, and individuals. The buyer of such a debt security has in effect lent money to the Treasury. The security is the lender's evidence that the government promises to pay off the debt at a certain date and to pay interest at a specified rate until then.

Bills, Notes and Bonds

The primary types of government securities are Treasury *bills*, *notes* and *bonds*. Putting aside minor differences, what distinguishes these from each other is simply the length of time for which they run. Treasury *bills* represent borrowing that the Treasury will repay in 1 year or less; *notes* represent debt due in between 2 and 10 years; and *bonds* are for debt running more than 10 years, and sometimes as much as 30 years.

Professionals often refer to all of these simply as *Treasuries*. Rather than specifying bills, notes, or bonds, they will talk about 1-month Treasuries, 2-year Treasuries, 20-year Treasuries, etc.

Maturity

Why the variety of Treasuries? There are two basic reasons. First, with over $2,000 billion of debt outstanding, it's obviously vital to the U.S. government to make sure that not too big a slice of the debt comes due at any one time. So the *maturities*—the dates when the debt securities become due—are intentionally scattered out as broadly as possible over a total 30-year period.

Variety

Second, in order to borrow and reborrow on this scale, the government has to consider the preferences of investors. Some investors will only lend their money out for short periods, such as 90 days. Others are happy buying a 20-year or 30-year bond. Many institutions have reason to want to own a whole range of Treasury securities, from the shortest to the longest. By offering something for everyone, the government gives itself the widest access to investors.

The wide range of offerings works well for both sides. From your point of view, it means that the list of government securities gives you all the choice and variety of maturities that you could possibly need or want.

Liquidity

What also gives great flexibility to the system is that the debt securities are fully *negotiable*, that is, they are a liquid investment that can be bought and sold easily. If you have bought $10,000 worth of a 20-year Treasury bond, and a year later find that you want to take your money out, you can't sell your bond back to the Treasury—the Treasury only pays off at the maturity date—but you can very easily sell it to another investor. In effect, he or she takes over your loan.

There's never any difficulty in selling a government security and getting your money out. (Normally, you are entitled to be paid on the business day following the sale.) Treasuries are traded in almost incredible volume among governments, banks, specialized Treasury securities dealers, other institutions and individuals. Every day, holders of Treasury securities who want to raise cash sell billions of dollars' worth of Treasuries to other investors who have extra cash to invest.

So when you lend to the U.S. government, you are not locked in. You can get out at any time by selling your loan to another lender. This is another reason why U.S. government securities are the world's favorite investment.

Other Government Securities

Treasury bills, notes and bonds are not the only U.S. government securities. There are also securities of various U.S. government agencies, such as the Federal Home Loan Banks, "Ginnie Mae," etc.; U.S. Savings Bonds (EE bonds and HH bonds); and some other variations. We'll discuss these other forms in Chapters 14–18.

4. ADVANTAGES OF TREASURIES

WHETHER OR NOT TREASURIES are the world's favorite investment, are they suitable for you? Needless to say, it depends on your individual needs and objectives. Let's consider more carefully what Treasuries can and can't do for you.

Safety

For many people, owning Treasuries, especially short-term Treasury bills, is seen as an alternative to keeping money in the bank. Let's look at this choice more closely.

Banks are usually viewed as safe, secure, convenient places to keep money. Each bank account is insured up to $100,000 by the Federal Deposit Insurance Corporation (FDIC) or, in the case of a savings and loan association, by the Federal Savings and Loan Insurance Corporation (FSLIC).

Critics sometimes point out that if many major banks were to fail at once, these agencies might not have the resources to pay off all depositors. We don't regard that as a practical problem. Such a massive, multiple bank failure seems extremely unlikely; and, even if it happened, we believe that the government would back up these insurance corporations with any resources needed to protect depositors.

But the banks still can't really match Treasuries for safety. First, while the government insurance on banks is limited to $100,000 per account, Treasuries will give you complete safety up to any amount. That may not be a problem for the average investor, but it's worth mentioning.

There's another point that is more relevant to the average bank depositor. If a bank *does* fail (and it sometimes happens), the fact that your account is below $100,000 doesn't mean that you are completely free from trouble.You can be sure of being paid off, but it's possible that your account could first be frozen for some time while the FDIC or FSLIC cleans up the mess. This tie-up could be inconvenient or even, in an extreme case, disastrous. We're not suggesting that you need to be nervous about leaving money in the bank, if you have reason to believe that the bank is well managed. But when it comes to complete safety, there's no doubt that Treasuries have the edge.

Liquidity

We've mentioned how *liquid* Treasuries are as an investment. Making comparison again with the banks, it's possible to argue that the banks have the edge in this respect. When you sell Treasuries (see Chapters 5 and 6), you have to wait a day before you can get a check. On the other hand, if you have money in a bank account, you can walk in any day and get your money on demand.

True, but that's not the full story. A bank money market deposit account (or market rate account) does make your money available on demand, but the interest rate you are paid is probably somewhat lower than you might earn by having your money invested in Treasury bills.

Moreover, consider what happens if you are willing to tie your money up for a longer period in order to earn a higher interest rate. A bank will offer you certificates of deposit (CDs) running from six months up to four or five years or more—the longer the CD, the higher the interest rate. However, there's a "substantial penalty for early withdrawal"—you lose substantial interest if you take your money out before the CD is due. To get the higher interest rate, you have given up a degree of *liquidity*.

With Treasuries, you have more flexibility. Here, too, you can earn a higher interest rate by moving out from the short-term Treasury bills to, let's say, a 3-year note, and still higher by moving out further to a long-term bond. But any of these securities, even the longest-term bond, can be sold in the market at any time, with your money available one day later.

The way the market mechanism works carries another advantage. You earn interest on your Treasuries for the exact number of days you own them, no more, no less. There's no waiting for a CD to mature, no waiting for bank interest to be credited at the end of a quarter, or any such complication. With Treasuries, you earn interest for whatever number of days your money is invested; it's as simple as that.

PART II
HOW TO
BUY AND
SELL TREASURIES

5·BUYING AND SELLING
TREASURY BILLS

WE'VE DISCUSSED THE TREMENDOUSLY active markets for Treasury securities, and the great liquidity they provide. You can easily buy bills, notes or bonds through a broker or bank; hold them for anywhere from a few days to several years; sell them when you wish, or hold them to maturity; and earn the interest for the exact number of days you hold them.

While most investors buy and sell Treasuries through brokers or banks, it's also possible to save commissions by buying new Treasury issues directly from the Treasury or through the regional Federal Re-

11

serve banks and branches. The procedures aren't difficult, and later in this chapter we'll explain how to go about it.

Buying Previously Issued Treasury Bills

For anyone with more than $10,000 to invest, Treasury bills—often called T-bills for short—are a popular short-term investment. The Treasury regularly sells bills in maturities of 3, 6 and 12 months. Bills come in a minimum denomination of $10,000 and in multiples of $5,000 above that figure.

Commissions

At any given time there are about 30 different Treasury bill issues available in the market, with maturities ranging from one week to one year. If you have $10,000 or more to invest and know when you will want to take it out, you can tailor your purchase by buying bills that come due at that date or slightly before. This kind of tailoring saves you commissions, since you normally pay a commission if you raise cash by selling bills before they mature, but there's usually no commission or fee for redeeming them at maturity.

How Banks and Brokers Charge

Banks and brokers charge varying amounts for transactions in Treasuries. The commission may be as low as $2.50 or even $1.25 per $1,000 face value, but there is likely to be a minimum charge, perhaps between $25 and $35. If you expect to do frequent transactions, you should certainly comparison shop regarding commission schedules.

Your bank or broker usually executes your trade (i.e., fills your buy or sell order) by going to one of the dealers who *make markets* in Treasury securities, buying and selling them regularly on demand. Your order is filled, and you are charged a commission or fee for the service. (For more general information on the securities markets, see the No Nonsense Financial Guide, *Understanding the Stock Market.*)

However, if you buy or sell through a bank or large brokerage firm that itself makes markets in Treasuries, there may be no stated commission. Instead, the bank or broker may sell Treasuries directly to you if you wish to buy, or buy them from you if you wish to sell. In this case, the fee for the service is usually built into the price.

Buying New Bill Issues

The above refers to transactions in Treasury bills that are already issued and on the market. You can also buy *new* T-bill issues (and, as we shall see later, new note and bond issues) through your broker or bank.

Auctions of 3-month and 6-month T-bills

Every Monday the Treasury conducts an auction sale of 3-month and 6-month bills. It's a real auction: the Treasury takes bids from banks and other large buyers, and accepts the bids that give the Treasury the best deal—that is, those at the lowest interest rates. Your bank or broker will probably take orders to buy bills "on the auction" up until Monday morning. The bills are actually issued and begin to earn interest on the following Thursday.

You don't have to worry about the auction aspect of the sale. As a smaller buyer, your order is entered on a noncompetitive basis, which means that you buy bills automatically at whatever is the average interest rate that the Treasury pays on this sale.

Auction of 12-month T-bills

You can buy 3-month bills if you will need the money soon. Otherwise, the 6-month bill will give you a slightly higher interest rate, and you will be able to wait longer before bothering with a renewal. If you want a still longer-term bill, usually carrying a somewhat higher rate of interest, auctions of 12-month bills are held every four weeks on a Thursday, with the bills issued the following Thursday.

Advantages of Auction Buying

There are two possible advantages to buying T-bills on the auction rather than in the open market. First, you may get a slightly higher interest rate than if you bought an existing issue in the market. Second, your broker or bank may charge a lower fee or commission for ordering bills on the auction than for buying them in the open market.

Discount Brokers

Incidentally, when it comes to buying and selling Treasuries, it's not clear that a discount broker will be cheaper than a traditional full-service broker. Both types are likely to charge minimum commissions that affect many transactions in Treasuries. You'll need to ask regarding commission schedules, and also regarding any additional fees or service charges that you may have to pay. In many cases there will be a fee for keeping custody of your Treasuries, but keep in mind that one of the prime advantages of using a bank or broker is the ability to leave the securities in custody of the broker, both for safety and easy resale. (For more information, see the No Nonsense Financial Guide, *How to Choose a Discount Stockbroker*.)

Buying New Bills Directly

If you are intent on saving fees and commissions, you can buy new Treasury bill issues *directly*, without any commission, through the regional Federal Reserve banks or through the Bureau of the Public Debt, U.S. Treasury.

If you decide to go this route, you'll find that both the Treasury and the Federal Reserve banks are organized to be helpful and encouraging. A list of the Federal Reserve banks and branches is included at the end of this book as Appendix A. For useful literature and order forms, contact your nearest Federal Reserve bank or branch or write to the Bureau of the Public Debt, Washington, DC 20226.

14

How to Bid on the Auction Yourself

You can buy Treasury bills on the auction by submitting either a *competitive* or a *noncompetitive* bid. Competitive bids, as mentioned earlier, are for banks and other large buyers who specify the percentage yield they are willing to accept. Their orders may or may not be filled, depending on the result of the auction. You will want to submit a *noncompetitive* bid, which means that you agree to buy bills at the *average interest rate* or *yield* of the accepted competitive tenders. (The Treasury first accepts the tenders specifying the lowest yield, and then moves up the scale until it has sold the total dollar amount of bills it is aiming for.)

You can usually submit a tender in person at one of the Reserve Banks up until 1:00 P.M. on the day of the auction. If you are mailing a noncompetitive tender, it must be postmarked by midnight of the day before the auction, and must be received by the Reserve Bank by the issue date.

You must enclose payment for the *full face value of the bills* ($10,000, $15,000, etc.). After the auction, you will receive a "discount check" for the difference between the face value and the actual purchase price. This check also is your evidence that your bid has been accepted, until you receive a statement 4 to 6 weeks later.

Your payment can be by (a) certified check made payable to the appropriate Federal Reserve bank or the Bureau of the Public Debt, (b) bank cashier's check, (c) Treasury securities maturing on or before the issue date of the new bills, or (d) a Treasury check for matured Treasury securities (but only if made out to your exact name, as on your purchase order).

You also need to enclose IRS Form W-9, which certifies your taxpayer identification number (Social Security number). The newest official tender forms incorporate the W-9 form. An important detail: the Treasury will withhold 20% of your interest earnings unless you check the box on this form certifying that you are *not* subject to "backup withholding." Check the box unless the IRS has notified you that you *are* subject to such withholding, which would only be in case of some past tax delinquency.

Your order can be submitted on an official tender form or by letter. If by letter, you need to specify the following: (a) your name, address, Social Security number and daytime telephone number, (b) the face amount of the bills you want to buy, (c) the maturity of the bills, (d) whether you are submitting a noncompetitive or competitive bid, and (e) whether you want to have your money automatically invested in new bills when these bills mature.

If you have not requested reinvestment, and if you have not transferred the bills to a bank or broker (see Chapter 11), the Treasury will mail you a check automatically for the face value of your bills when they mature. The interest you have earned is the difference between this face value and your original cost (see Chapter 8).

6·BUYING AND SELLING TREASURY NOTES AND BONDS

TREASURY NOTES AND BONDS are bought and sold in much the same way as bills, but with some variations.

Notes are generally sold with maturities of 2 to 10 years, bonds for more than 10 years. Notes maturing in less than 4 years are sold in minimum denominations of $5,000, while longer notes and bonds are issued in denominations of $1,000 and up.

How Interest Is Paid

Unlike bills, Treasury notes and bonds pay interest semi-annually at the rate stated on the security. Interest is payable on the day and month corresponding to the maturity date, and 6 months later. For example, the 10¼% Treasury bonds that mature on May 15, 2003, pay interest regularly every May 15 and November 15.

Commissions

Like Treasury bills, existing issues of notes and bonds can easily be bought and sold in the market through your bank or broker. By custom, commissions are likely to be higher than on bills. Brokers usually charge more on longer notes and bonds than on shorter maturities, not because it costs more to execute the transaction, but because it's assumed that the customer will be more willing to pay a commission on a security that he or she plans to hold for a longer period of time.

On a longer bond, a commission of $5 per $1,000 is not unreasonable (with a minimum of perhaps $25 or

17

$30 per transaction). But there should also be a *maximum* limit on the commission. If you are fortunate enough to deal in $50,000 or $100,000 of Treasuries at a clip, there's no reason why you should pay a commission of more than $150, or at the most $200, on a single transaction.

Buying New Notes and Bonds

You can subscribe to new Treasury note and bond offerings in much the same way as you subscribe to new bills. Generally, the Treasury issues new 2-year notes at the end of each month, and new 4-year notes in March, June, September and December. Longer notes and bonds are issued irregularly, but you can obtain information on future offerings by contacting your local Federal Reserve bank or branch.

As with bills, you can submit a noncompetitive bid and be sure of buying the securities at the average price paid in the auction.

Payment

A difference in the case of notes and bonds is that your payment check need not be certified—an ordinary personal check will do. There will almost certainly be a small price adjustment after the auction. Because of the auction process, notes and bonds are usually sold either at a slight discount (less than face value) or at a slight premium (more than face value). If the auction results in a discount, a check for the difference will be mailed to you on the issue date. If the sale is at a premium, you will be notified and must pay the additional amount before the issue date.

An important difference is in the *form* of the security you are buying. Treasury bills are held in a Treasury book-entry account, and you receive only a statement of your account. But when you buy notes or bonds directly on the offering, you receive actual certificates for the notes or bonds, registered in your name. You can hold these, or deposit them with your bank or broker, or sell them through a bank or broker.

18

Your bid must specify whether you want the securities mailed to you (which usually takes place within 4 weeks of the issue date) or whether you wish to pick them up at your Federal Reserve bank or branch. You must also specify where you want your interest checks mailed; if you wish, this can be to your bank rather than to you directly.

When your notes or bonds mature, you can redeem them through a bank or broker (who may charge a fee), or by submitting them directly to your Federal Reserve bank. They can be used to pay for new securities, or you can receive a check on the maturity date.

PART III
THINGS YOU NEED TO KNOW

7·UNDERSTANDING YIELDS AND PRICES

The Importance of Yield

Bonds, notes and bills are all, as we have said, *debt* securities. This means that they are *fixed-income* securities on which the investor's objective is to receive a certain stated interest rate return.

In buying any fixed-income security, the most critical figure for the investor is the *yield*. From your standpoint, the yield is the interest rate *you* will earn by buying a security.

We're all familiar with the concept of yield. We talk about earning 6% on our money, or 8%, or 12%.

For the investor who lives on the income from investments, yield is what determines the amount of spendable income. For the investor who plows back

21

income into the account, yield determines the rate at which your money will grow.

In a bank account, your yield is simple. It depends on what interest rate the bank is paying for that day, or month, or year.

Yield is also simple in a money market fund. You buy *shares* in the fund, but the shares are almost always priced at $1.00, and you figure your yield, basically, as if the money were in a bank. (See the No Nonsense Financial Guide, *Understanding Money Market Funds*.)

When Yield Becomes Complicated

However, when you buy most debt securities, the yield may not be figured that simply. The yield depends not only on the stated interest rate of the security, but also on the *price* you pay.

Let's say that you buy a $1,000 Treasury bond, due in 10 years and paying 8%. If the stated interest rate is 8%, the bond is said to be carrying an "8% coupon." Your interest on the bond is $80 (8% times $1,000), and this would be paid in two semiannual installments of $40 each.

If you pay exactly $1,000 to buy the bond, you are said to be buying it at *par*, and your *current yield*—that is, your immediate rate of return on the bond—is figured as follows:

$$\text{current yield} = \frac{\text{annual interest (in \$)}}{\text{price or cost (in \$)}} = \frac{\$80}{\$1,000} = 8\%$$

Because you bought the bond at par, your yield is the same as the stated interest rate on the bond. But what if you had bought the bond in the market for $900? Then your current yield would be $80/$900 = 8.89%, considerably more than the stated interest rate on the bond. Or if you had paid $1,100 for the bond, your current yield would be $80/$1,100 = 7.27%.

For practice, check these on your calculator. Because it is so important, we will repeat: on a debt security, the *yield* you earn depends on both the *stated interest rate* of the security and the *price* you pay.

Yield to Maturity

We've talked above about *current* yield. You need also to understand the concept of *yield to maturity*.

In the example above of a 10-year, 8% bond bought for $900, we disregarded the fact that in 10 years, the bond will be paid off at its face value of $1,000. So in addition to the current yield of 8.89%, the buyer will get a profit of $100 after 10 years. In the other case of a bond bought at $1,100, the buyer will suffer a *loss* of $100 at the end of the 10th year.

Since most previously issued bonds sell in the market at either above or below $1,000, a buyer can almost always foresee some profit or loss at the maturity date, when the bond is paid off (redeemed) at $1,000.

The concept of yield to maturity takes this profit or loss into account. By a rather complicated formula, an adjustment is made to the current yield figure. This adjustment reflects the expected profit or loss to be realized when the bond matures, and the *time* that will elapse before that happens. The resulting figure—the yield to maturity—is accepted everywhere by bond investors as the fullest and fairest measure of the return you will earn when you buy a debt security.

In the above examples, the 10-year, 8% bond bought for $900, with a *current yield* of 8.89%, would have a *yield to maturity* of 9.58%, with the expected profit taken into account. On the other hand, the same bond bought for $1,100, with a current yield of 7.27%, would have a yield to maturity of only 6.62%, after adjusting for the expected loss.

The actual formula for calculating yield to maturity is complicated. Professionals use yield tables, and there are several small calculators on the market with financial programs that include yield to maturity.

You may attach importance to *current yield*, as the measure of the immediate income you will get from an investment. But *yield to maturity* is the full measure of what you will get by buying a note or bond, and it is the measure to use in making serious comparisons of one fixed-income investment against another.

Prices and Yields of Notes and Bonds

The market prices of Treasuries are published daily in the *Wall Street Journal* and most major newspapers. Some explanation will probably be helpful.

Prices of Treasury notes and bonds are usually combined in a single table. First, for those who are not familiar with bond price quotations: even though $1,000 is considered the basic unit of denomination in bonds and notes, all bond and note *prices* are expressed on the basis of *100*, which is often referred to as *par*.

You multiply the price by ten to find the actual value of a $1,000 bond. A bond at *par* is selling exactly for its face value of $1,000; at "par and a half" it is selling for 100½, or $1,005. A price of 98 means that a $1,000 note or bond is selling for $980; a price of 112 would mean $1,120.

Note also that while prices of corporate and tax-exempt bonds are usually expressed in points and eighths of a point, prices of government bonds and notes are expressed in points and *thirty-seconds* of a point to permit more sensitive adjustments. And to confuse the unwary, these are written just as if they were decimals. So 101.2 means 101²⁄₃₂, and so on. Now you know why those "decimals" in the Treasury price tables never go higher than .31—in case you ever noticed.

Since you have to convert the thirty-seconds into real decimals for all calculations, and since you may not carry the decimal equivalents of thirty-seconds around in your head, we have listed them at the end of this chapter.

The daily price listings show about 150 different issues of Treasury bonds and notes. On the following page are a few typical listings showing the prices of June 30, 1987, as published in the *Wall Street Journal*.

The listings are not really complicated. For example: the 7⅞% notes due in June 1991 (the small letter "n" indicates a note) were quoted at 99²⁵⁄₃₂

Rate		Mat. Date		Bid	Asked	Bid chg.	Yld.
6 ⅛s	1989	Jan	n	98.7	98.11	+ .2	7.25
10 ¾s	1990	Aug	n	107.30	108.2	− .1	7.79
7 ⅞s	1991	June	n	99.25	99.27	− .2	7.92
7 ¼s	1992	Aug		99.5	99.13	− .2	7.39
10 ⅛s	1993	May	n	108.27	108.31	− .5	8.17
10 ⅛s	1994	Nov		109.22	109.30	− .24	8.30
8 ½s	1994-99	May		99.22	100.6	− .16	8.46
11 ⅞s	2003	Nov		126.20	126.28	− .9	8.75
12s	2008-13	Aug		130.6	130.10	− .10	8.81
8¾s	2017	May		102.20	102.22	− .5	8.50

Read "s" as a % sign, e.g. 10⅛s = 10⅛%.
"n"—notes.
"Mat. Date"—maturity date.
"Bid chg."—change in bid price from previous day.
"Yld."—yield to maturity.
Where two years are shown under maturity date, the bond matures in the later year but is *callable* beginning in the earlier year. (See Chapter 10.)

bid, 99²⁷⁄₃₂ asked, down ²⁄₃₂ from the day before. The bid price is the price at which a dealer offers to buy a security; the asked price is the price at which a dealer offers to sell a security. So when you buy a security, you basically pay the "asked" price. At a price of 99.27, the *yield to maturity* of these notes was 7.92%.

If you had bought the 11⅞% bonds due in November 2003 at the dealer price, you would have paid 126²⁸⁄₃₂. In decimal terms, that's 126.875, which works out to $1,268.75 per $1,000 bond. Because of the high price, your yield to maturity would have been only 8.75%.

Actually, when you buy or sell Treasury bonds or notes, you won't get the dealer prices shown in the paper, unless you are buying and selling in amounts of $1 million or more. But the difference shouldn't be great. If you are more than ¼ point (⁸⁄₃₂) away from the dealer price, you have a right to ask your bank or broker why. Also remember that as a retail buyer or seller, as pointed out previously, you will probably have to pay a commission.

Decimal Equivalents of 32nds

32nds	Fractional Equivalent	Decimal Equivalent	32nds	Fractional Equivalent	Decimal Equivalent
1	$1/32$	.03125	17	$17/32$	.53125
2	$1/16$	.0625	18	$9/16$	.5625
3		.09375	19		.59375
4	$1/8$	.125	20	$5/8$	.625
5		.15625	21		.65625
6	$3/16$	.1875	22	$11/16$	.6875
7		.21875	23		.71875
8	$1/4$	.25	24	$3/4$	.75
9		.28125	25		.78125
10	$5/16$	.3125	26	$13/16$	.8125
11		.34375	27		.84375
12	$3/8$	.375	28	$7/8$	.875
13		.40625	29		.90625
14	$7/16$	.4375	30	$15/16$	.9375
15		.46875	31		.96875
16	$1/2$	.50	32	1	1.00

8·PRICES AND YIELDS OF TREASURY BILLS

Prices of Treasury Bills

The prices of Treasury bills are quoted not on the basis of *price*, but on the basis of *yield*—that is, on the basis of the interest rate you will earn if you buy the bills and hold them to maturity. A typical newspaper listing might look like this, with the various bill issues listed, from the issue that matures in the next week to the longest issue maturing in about a year:

Prices of U.S. Treasury Bills
June 30, 1987

Mat. date	Bid	Asked	Yield
	% Discount %		%
1987			
7-2	4.01	3.55	0.00
7-9	5.51	5.45	5.53
7-16	5.18	5.04	5.12
7-23	5.07	5.01	5.09
7-30	4.89	4.81	4.90
8-6	5.38	5.34	5.44
8-13	5.38	5.36	5.47
8-20	5.41	5.37	5.48
8-27	5.40	5.32	5.44
9-3	5.64	5.58	5.71
9-10	5.60	5.54	5.68
9-17	5.64	5.60	5.75
9-24	5.65	5.61	5.76
10-1	5.73	5.71	5.87
10-8	5.71	5.67	5.84
10-15	5.73	5.67	5.85
10-22	5.72	5.68	5.86

Mat. date	Bid	Asked	Yield
	% Discount %		%
10-29	5.83	5.77	5.96
11-5	5.84	5.78	5.98
11-12	5.86	5.82	6.04
11-19	5.98	5.94	6.17
11-27	5.90	5.84	6.07
12-3	5.95	5.91	6.15
12-10	5.91	5.87	6.11
12-17	5.94	5.90	6.15
12-24	5.96	5.92	6.18
1988			
1-21	5.86	5.82	6.08
2-18	6.09	6.03	6.32
3-17	6.14	6.10	6.41
4-14	6.18	6.14	6.47
5-12	6.29	6.27	6.63
6-9	6.30	6.28	6.67

"Mat. date"—maturity date
"Discount"—means that bid and asked prices are on discounted basis.

The left-hand column lists the bill issues coming due over the next year, from the nearest to the farthest. The next two columns show bid and asked prices for each issue. These are the prices for the previous day quoted by professional dealers for large-scale trades.

These were prices in effect on June 30, 1987. Look at the bill issue of October 1, which at that time was due to mature in about 90 days. Bid means that dealers were willing to buy that issue at a price representing a yield of 5.73% to maturity on October 1. The asked price means that they were willing to *sell* the same issue at a price equivalent to a yield of 5.71%. If you were an institution buying bills in large quantities (in this market, "large" means $1 million or more), you could have bought bills on June 30, due to mature on October 1, at a price giving you a yield of 5.71%.

If you are used to stock price quotations such as "bid 30, asked 31," it may seem upside down to see "bid 5.73, asked 5.71." But remember that yields move *inversely* or *opposite* to price. Think about this a minute, and you will see that it makes sense. When you buy a debt security, the higher the *price* you pay, the lower the *yield* on your money. And vice versa.

Discounted Yield and True Yield

You'll notice that there's a third price column, headed "Yield." Why? The reason is that while T-bill prices are quoted based on *yield*, they are not quoted at what would be considered *true yield*, but rather at a somewhat different figure called *discounted yield*.

To explain, we'll oversimplify some of the details. Let's say that you buy a 91-day Treasury bill at a quoted yield of 8.00%. The 8.00% represents yield for a full year, and you will only own the bill for ¼ year, so your actual yield for the 91 days is 2.00%. On a $1,000 bill, 2.00% is equal to $20. Since Treasury bills are sold on a *discount* basis, the dealer subtracts $20 from $1,000 and sells you the bill for $980.

Ninety-one days later, you redeem your bill for $1,000. You have earned $20 in interest ($1,000 minus $980). But since you only put up $980 to buy the bill, your real yield is not $20/$1,000 = 2.00%, but rather $20/$980 = 2.04%. And on an annual basis, you've earned not 8.00%, but 8.16%.

This is why the true yield on T-bills (sometimes referred to as *coupon yield* or *bond-equivalent yield*) is different from discounted yield. In the above example, the difference isn't great. But it becomes greater with 6-month bills and much greater with 1-year bills. The "Yield" column shows the *true yield* equivalent of the asked price; it's a better measure of what you will actually earn on your money.

Basis Points

You'll note that the interest rates are quoted in decimals—5.73%, 5.71%, etc. In professional parlance, ¹⁄₁₀₀ of 1% is a *"basis point."* This saves a lot of words. For example, in the quotation above of 5.73% bid, 5.71% asked, you could say that the *spread* of .02% between bid and asked is 2 *basis points*. Price changes on bills are most often expressed in terms of basis points.

Some newspapers include a "Change" or "Chg." column in the table of bill prices. This simply represents the change in the quoted asked price from the day previous. If the asked price is 5.71%, and the day before it was 5.65%, the "Change" column would show "+0.06," and dealers would say that the bills were "up 6 basis points."

What Price on a New Issue?

If you are subscribing to a new Treasury bill issue, either through your bank or broker or directly through the Federal Reserve, you can't tell precisely what the yield on your bills will be. As we've said, the Treasury sells bills every week on an *auction* basis, which means that it sells the bills to whichever banks and other buyers will accept the lowest yields.

However, bill yields don't usually change sharply from day to day or even from week to week, and you can get a close idea of the yield you will get by looking at the yields on bills shown in the latest newspaper quotations. The 91-day issue should sell at about the same yield as existing bills due in three months, and the 182-day issue should sell at about the same yield as existing bills due in six months, unless there's been some substantial change in the market. And if you're buying a new issue of 1-year bills, the yield should be close to that of the existing bills coming due in about 11 months.

Actually, in the case of a new issue, your yield may be a little better than that on the existing issues. In order to get a new issue of several billion dollars out into the market successfully, the Treasury often has to pay a small fraction more in yield than the current quotation on comparable bills.

Wholesale and Retail

If you are buying or selling previously issued bills, remember that, just as in the case of bonds and notes, the quoted prices in the newspaper are the prices at which dealers trade large quantities with each other or with institutions. If you go into the market through your bank or broker to buy or sell $10,000 or $25,000 of bills, you won't get those prices. You will pay a slightly higher price (and get a slightly lower yield) on the asked side if you are buying, and you will receive a slightly lower price on the bid side if you are selling.

The premium you pay on retail quantities is only a few basis points, and you shouldn't let it disturb you. The dealers don't make much money on small transactions. A spread of 4 basis points on a $10,000 purchase and sale of 90-day bills would give the dealer a trading profit of about *$1.00*, which shows just how narrow those trading spreads really are. Even the somewhat larger spread that will be charged on your transaction probably won't be enough to pay for the paperwork on the trade.

9·INTEREST AND ACCRUED INTEREST

BEFORE WE LEAVE THE subject of interest and yield, there are a few more points you need to know—particularly when figuring your interest received for income tax purposes.

Calculating Interest on Treasury Bills

Interest on Treasury bills is calculated simply by taking the net amount you receive from selling or redeeming them, and subtracting your cost. Under the tax law, there's never a capital gain on a Treasury bill. Whatever you get is interest. If you buy a Treasury bill for $960, and sell it a month later for $970, you've earned $10 interest. When doing this calculation, any commission you paid to purchase the bills is included in the cost; and any commission you paid to sell the bills is deducted from the proceeds. (Of course, if the bills have been held to maturity and redeemed, there's no sales commission.)

Interest on Notes and Bonds

As explained previously, notes and bonds pay interest semiannually—on the day and month corresponding to the maturity date, and 6 months later. If your notes or bonds are being held for you by a bank or broker, the interest will be credited to your account, or mailed out to you, depending on the arrangement you have made. If you have bought the securities direct and they are registered with the Treasury under your own name, you will receive your interest checks directly from the Treasury.

For Treasury bills, as we've explained, there's no separate interest mailing or crediting. The Treasury pays off the bills at face value on maturity, and your interest is the difference between the face value ($1,000 per bill) and your cost.

The Accrued Interest Adjustment

When you buy previously issued bonds or notes in the market, your purchase date almost always falls somewhere in between the semiannual interest dates. This means that when the next interest date arrives, you will receive 6 months' interest, even if you have only owned the bonds or notes for 5 months, or 1 month, or for as little as a day.

To make this work out fairly for both buyer and seller, bonds and notes are traded with *accrued interest*. When you make your purchase, you pay the seller an additional amount to compensate for the interest he or she is losing, based on the number of days from the last interest date to the date of sale. Your purchase confirmation on notes or bonds should show the principal cost of the securities, plus any commission, plus the accrued interest you have paid.

In this case, the 6 months' interest payment that you will receive is reported in full for income tax purposes. But the accrued interest you paid is shown as a *deduction* from interest received.

(If you need to adjust for accrued interest paid, you must file your federal income tax return on Form 1040, not Form 1040A or Form 1040EZ. On Schedule B of Form 1040, below your list of items of interest income received, enter the item, "Less: accrued interest paid," as a negative item which is then subtracted from your interest income. Make this adjustment in the first year when you actually receive an interest payment on the bonds, even if you bought the bonds in the previous year.)

When you *sell* notes or bonds in the market, the procedure is reversed. Now, in addition to the base sales price, you *receive* accrued interest based on the number of days you have held the security since the last interest date. This accrued interest received is shown as an additional item of interest income on your tax schedule.

Let us say again that this is one of the great advantages of Treasuries. Whether you buy bills, notes or bonds, you earn interest for the exact number of days you own them—from time of purchase to time of sale or redemption. No fuss—no problem—no minimum period that you must leave your money in—no substantial penalty for early withdrawal. If you can deal in the quantities involved, you couldn't ask for a better arrangement.

10·CALLABILITY: AN IMPORTANT NON-PROBLEM

ONE OF THE ADVANTAGES of government bonds is that they are, to a great extent, *noncallable*. Let us explain what this is and why it's an advantage.

Most corporate and tax-exempt bonds are *callable*. After they have been out a certain number of years (perhaps 5 or 10 years), the issuing corporation or local government has the right to *call* them, that is to redeem them early, that is, well before maturity.

This almost always works to the disadvantage of you, the bondholder. When does an issuer choose to call a bond issue? When interest rates have dropped and the issuer can replace the old bond issue with a new issue at a lower interest rate. So the issuer pays you your money back, and then, if you want to replace the bond, you have to buy a new bond carrying a lower interest rate.

There's no such problem with government bonds, or at least the problem is so minor as to be unimportant. Many government bonds are *noncallable* before maturity. Others can be called, but only within the 5 years just before the maturity date, which keeps the problem within manageable proportions.

Look at the newspaper price quotations for Treasury bonds and notes on page 25, and you'll see that many of the longer-term issues are listed with what appear to be two maturity dates, five years apart. This actually refers to callability. For instance, the 12% bonds of August 2008–2013, are due in August 2013, but can be called at the option of the Treasury at any time beginning August 2008.

The noncallability of Treasury bonds greatly increases your potential for making profits on swings in the bond market. In the 1980–82 period, when interest rates were very high, the Treasury issued some bonds at interest rates ranging to over 15%. In mid-1985, when interest rates on new bonds were much lower, these issues with very high coupons (that is, high stated interest rates) sold at high premiums. Various issues were selling in the market at prices of from roughly 120 to 135, or from $1,200 to $1,350 per bond—that is, $200 to $350 above the original offering price of $1,000 per bond, representing a profit of 20% to 35%.

If these had been corporate or tax-exempt bonds, the bonds would very likely have been callable after 5 or 10 years at a price not far above the $1,000 face value. Because of the likelihood of a call, investors would not have been willing to pay a big premium for the bonds, and market prices would not have been nearly so high.

To attract bond buyers, some corporate and tax-exempt issues in recent years have been made non-callable, or callable only after many years, or callable only at a high premium. But when it comes to callability, Treasuries still generally give investors by far the best break.

11·FORMS OF OWNERSHIP

THE MOST FLEXIBLE WAY to own Treasury bills, notes and bonds is to buy them through a bank or broker, and leave them on deposit there. Many investors feel that the flexibility and convenience are well worth the small commissions involved.

If you want to sell Treasuries before they mature, you *must* do it through a bank or a broker.

Brokers and banks establish their own rules regarding accounts, and the rules vary. Ordinarily, of course, you will be better off dealing with an institution that already knows you. But make sure you know the answers to the following questions:

- What fee will you be charged for subscribing to a new T-bill issue? Or new notes or bonds?
- What commissions or fees will you pay for buying or selling T-bills in the open market? Or notes or bonds?
- Are there fees for holding Treasuries in the account, or any other account fees?
- If you are buying, when will your payment be due at the bank or broker? On settlement date (usually one day after trade date), or before the trade is made?
- If you sell Treasuries in the account, when will you be able to get your cash?
- Are there any limitations on how the account may be registered?
- What are the procedures for placing buy and sell orders?

As we said in Chapter 5, a discount broker won't necessarily be cheaper than a full-service broker for transactions in Treasuries. You will have to shop around.

Usually you can register a brokerage account in any of the ways customary in the securities industry—

in individual name or joint names (either as joint tenants with right of survivorship, or as tenants in common), or as a custodian account for a minor, etc. You can place your buy or sell orders by telephone, and your work is kept to a minimum.

When You Buy Treasuries Directly

If you are saving commissions by buying Treasuries directly through a Federal Reserve bank, you won't have the same flexibility.

T-bills

As for bills, the Treasury issues bills only in book-entry form, which means that ownership is evidenced by entries on the Treasury's records, without the issuance of any certificates. You receive a statement of your account (just as you might from a bank or broker), perhaps 4 to 6 weeks after the bills are issued.

The Treasury doesn't want to be bothered recording changes of ownership, and it urges that bills be bought directly through the Federal Reserve banks only if you plan to hold them to maturity. You can transfer your bills to an account at a bank or broker (where they can then be sold)—but not in the first 20 days after purchase, and not in the last 20 days before maturity. Don't count on your money being quickly available, except at maturity.

Notes or Bonds

If you buy Treasury notes or bonds directly, you also have limited liquidity. Your certificate evidencing ownership of the notes or bonds is mailed to you (or can be picked up at your Federal Reserve bank), usually by 4 weeks after the issue date. You can then sell the security by delivering the certificate to a bank or broker. But your money has been effectively locked up from the purchase date until the time you receive the certificate; and your payment on the sale may be delayed by the time required to get ownership transferred out of your name.

Bearer Securities

Years ago, it was possible to buy Treasury securities in bearer form. Rather than being registered in anyone's name, these securities were freely negotiable like currency, and were submitted for redemption by whoever held them at maturity. The semiannual interest on these bearer notes and bonds was obtained by clipping coupons attached to the security (one coupon for every interest date) and depositing them through a bank—which is why the stated interest rate on a bond is still referred to as the "coupon."

This was an obvious invitation to tax evasion, and the Treasury no longer issues bearer securities. But many of the old bearer notes and bonds are still outstanding. Now, however, when the owner of an old bearer note or bond deposits or cashes a semiannual interest coupon, he or she must provide a Social Security number to be recorded with the payment.

Leaving Securities in Street Name

When you leave your Treasury securities on deposit with a bank or broker, they are being held in *street name*. The Treasury does not have your name on file. The securities are ordinarily held in an account at one of the Federal Reserve banks under the name of the bank or broker, and your name appears only on the internal records maintained by the bank or broker.

As long as the bank or broker is reputable, and as long as you get a statement from the bank or broker confirming your ownership of the securities, this is a safe and reasonable arrangement.

SIPC Insurance

Some people worry about leaving securities with a broker. Historically, brokerage firms have not always been as safe as they should be. But accounts at brokerage firms are now insured up to $500,000 by the Securities Investor Protection Corporation (SIPC). If you have an account at a brokerage firm that fails, there may be a delay in getting control of your securities, but SIPC will save you from disaster.

In the next chapter we'll examine another reason for leaving Treasury securities in street name—the fact that you can *borrow* on them simply, quickly, and at low cost.

12·BORROWING ON YOUR TREASURIES

OWNING TREASURIES CAN BE a very favorable source of credit. Because Treasuries are the safest of all securities, banks will lend willingly against them as collateral, and the margin account rules permit brokers to lend against Treasuries on very favorable terms.

A carefully selected broker is likely to give you a better deal than most banks. If you think you may want to make this use of your Treasuries, you should shop for a broker who charges low interest rates, and then leave your Treasuries on deposit with that broker.

Margin Accounts

In a brokerage *margin account* you can usually borrow up to 50% of the market value of common stocks in the account, but up to *90%* of the market value of Treasuries. If your Treasuries are worth $20,000, for example, you have a completely flexible $18,000 credit line, and you are charged interest only on the exact amount you choose to borrow, and for the exact time that your borrowing is outstanding. It's one of the most flexible and effective forms of borrowing available to an individual.

It's also one of the cheapest. As to the interest charges, some brokers charge their customers as little as ½ of 1% above the *brokers' call loan rate*, which is the very low rate at which the broker is borrowing money from the banks. But some brokers take a much wider spread. Make sure you know what you will be charged, and whether there will be any other account charges that will increase your costs.

To show you how advantageous margin borrowing

can be: in early 1987, borrowing rates on mortgage loans were in the 9½-10% range, automobile loans were also averaging 9½-10%, and a cash advance on your Visa or MasterCard might have cost you anywhere from 15% to 20% at most banks. But the margin rate at certain brokers was as low as 8% or less. Leaving tax considerations aside, there was probably no other way in which the average individual could have done nearly as well. (For more on borrowing, see the No Nonsense Financial Guide, *How to Use Credit and Credit Cards*.)

When making interest rate comparisons, however, tax considerations now have to be taken into account. Before 1987, all interest payments were generally deductible in calculating your federal income tax. But the Tax Reform Act of 1986 has imposed critical distinctions. Interest on most *mortgage-type borrowings* remains generally tax-deductible. *Investment interest*— the interest paid on money borrowed to buy or carry securities or other investments—is deductible, but only against various types of *investment income*. Interest on other types of borrowings, categorized as "consumer interest," is basically *nondeductible*. (The deduction is being phased out over the five years 1987–1991.) So, if you borrow on your Treasuries, the deductibility of the interest you pay will depend on the purpose of the borrowings. If you borrow against Treasuries in a margin account to buy more Treasuries, or common stocks or other securities, the interest will be deductible against your investment income. But if you take the money out to buy a boat, the interest is likely to be classified as consumer interest.

If you do take advantage of your Treasuries to borrow, never lose sight of the fact that you are *pledging* your securities against the loan. The loan may be outstanding indefinitely, as long as you continue to pay the interest charges, and as long as the loan balance is no more than 90% of the market value of your Treasuries. But eventually, if you can't repay the loan, the Treasuries may have to be sold to provide repayment.

The moral: just because the borrowing power is there, don't make the mistake of using it carelessly.

13·HOW TREASURIES ARE TAXED

WHEN YOU OWN TREASURIES, you enjoy a tax advantage. The income on Treasury bills, notes and bonds is fully subject to federal income tax. But it is *exempt by law from all state and local income taxes.*

Most federal agency securities also enjoy the state and local income tax exemption. But there are exceptions. For example, the interest on Ginnie Mae (GNMA) certificates and Fannie Mae (FNMA) securities (see Chapter 14) is fully subject to state and local taxes.

Impact of the New Tax Law

By reducing federal income tax rates, the Tax Reform Act of 1986 has made the state and local tax exemption relatively more important to many investors.

An example will show why. Let's say you own fully taxable corporate bonds which yield interest on which you pay $100 of state income tax. Let's also assume that you itemize deductions on your federal tax return. Previously, if you were in the top 50% federal income tax bracket, deducting the $100 of state income tax on your federal return saved you $50 of federal tax. So the *net* cost to you of the $100 state tax was only $50.

But now, if your federal tax bracket drops to 28% or 33% under the new law, the deduction will save you only $28 or $33 of federal tax, and the net cost to you of the state tax will be $72 or $67, rather than $50. You can see why there may now be an additional incentive to switch from corporate bonds to Treasury bonds, which are fully exempt from the state income tax. Of course, the Treasury bonds will yield less than corporates, and we're not recommending that you make such a switch without taking all factors into account. But if you are paying heavy state and/or local income taxes on your interest income, think about Treasuries.

Your Federal Tax Return

As we said, all interest on Treasuries is subject to *federal* income tax and must be reported on your federal income tax return.

If you have more than $400 in interest income in a given year, you must file your federal income tax return on Form 1040A or Form 1040 (not Form 1040EZ).

Income on Treasury notes and bonds is reported in the year received. As we pointed out in Chapter 9, you should not neglect accrued interest adjustments on purchases or sales of notes or bonds, but should add them to, or subtract them from, your other income items. (Form 1040 is required if you wish to deduct accrued interest you have paid out on a bond purchase.)

Income on Treasury bills is reported in the year the bills *mature* or are *sold*. The refund check you receive shortly after your purchase when you buy bills directly is *not* interest, but an adjustment on your purchase price. As stated earlier, the interest you report on Treasury bills is simply the difference between your total cost to acquire the bills and your total proceeds when you dispose of them.

If you buy or sell Treasury notes or bonds in the open market, you will have a capital gain or loss when you sell or redeem them. This gain or loss must be reported on Schedule D of Form 1040. For this purpose, redemption of the securities at maturity is equivalent to a sale at face value. Beginning in 1988, capital gains are taxed at exactly the same rates as other types of income; for 1987, long-term capital gains retain a trace of their former preference, with the maximum rate on long-term gains fixed at 28%.

If you have bought notes or bonds at a price above or below face value, part of any gain or loss may be taxed as an interest item instead of a capital item. The rules are complex; consult your tax accountant, or the local IRS office.

How Treasuries Compare

The exemption from state and local taxes gives Treasuries a certain advantage over bank CDs, ordinary money market funds, and most other fixed-income investments.

As for federal income taxes, the effect of the 1986 Tax Reform Act is to put various types of investments on a more equal footing than before, so that choices will be made according to basic economic factors rather than because of tax advantages. Many tax-sheltered investments have been effectively eliminated. The tax preference on long-term capital gains, which previously gave common stocks and other "growth" investments an advantage over Treasuries for many investors, is being eliminated. These changes are likely to broaden the demand for Treasuries as an investment.

Many high-bracket investors will continue to favor tax-exempt (municipal) bonds—the bonds issued by state and local governments, which are largely exempt from federal income taxes. The relative attractiveness of tax-exempts as against Treasuries depends on the level of tax rates and on an individual's tax bracket, as well as on competitive prices and yields at any given time. With federal tax rates lower, tax-exempt bonds will have to provide yields closer to those on Treasuries in order to stay competitive in the market. (For more information, see the No Nonsense Financial Guide, *Understanding Tax-Exempt Bonds*.)

Gift and Estate Taxes

Government securities are fully subject to federal and state gift, estate and inheritance taxes. For the special advantage of certain Treasury bonds when paying estate taxes, see Chapter 17.

Keeping Records

It's important to keep accurate records of your Treasury transactions.

All statements from the Treasury or from your bank or broker showing how much interest you've earned should be kept carefully for tax purposes. On any purchases or sales of notes or bonds in the open market, keep records of the transaction, and note all *accrued interest* items.

If you have Treasury securities on deposit at a broker or bank, your year-end income statement for tax purposes (Form 1099) may not show interest on Treasuries separately from other interest. You will have to calculate how much of your total interest income came from Treasuries in order to exclude this amount when calculating state and local taxes.

Always keep your records of purchase of notes or bonds until the securities are sold or redeemed. In the year of sale or redemption, you will need to know your original purchase date and cost in order to report capital gain or loss and any interest adjustments. If you buy 10-year or 20-year Treasuries, make sure you have a good filing system for your cost records.

PART IV
SOME SPECIAL APPROACHES

14·GINNIE MAE AND OTHERS

IN ADDITION TO THE securities that are direct obligations of the U.S. Treasury, several government agencies issue their own securities to raise money for operations—the Federal Home Loan Banks, Federal Farm Credit System, etc.

Most of these are less important to the average investor than they used to be. Years ago, when yields on Treasuries were very low, there was a distinct advantage to a long-term investor in holding a comparable agency note or bond with a somewhat higher yield. But now, with interest rates higher and with the Treasury borrowing at astronomical levels, the rate differential is relatively less than it was.

Also, since the markets for agency securities are

somewhat less active, the cost of getting in and out of these securities in the open market is likely to be somewhat greater than with Treasuries.

Full Faith and Credit

Some agency securities carry the "full faith and credit" of the U.S. government—that is, they are fully guaranteed by the Treasury. Others are backed only by the credit of the individual agency. In theory this is a meaningful distinction, but on a practical basis we find it unthinkable that Congress would ever let a federal agency default.

Tax Advantages

Like the interest on Treasuries, the interest on most agency securities is exempt from state and local taxes. But there are exceptions, the most notable of which are the Federal National Mortgage Association (FNMA, or Fannie Mae) and the Government National Mortgage Association (GNMA, or Ginnie Mae).

There's some logic to these exceptions. While Fannie Mae is often regarded as a government agency, technically it is privately owned. And while the Ginnie Mae securities that have become popular are government-guaranteed, they are, as we shall see, quite different from a usual government security.

Ginnie Mae Certificates

Ginnie Maes have achieved status as the highest-yielding security carrying a full government guarantee. They are actually *mortgage pass-through certificates*. The holder receives monthly payments that represent a share in the principal-and-interest payments on a pool of government-guaranteed mortgages.

The advantages are the high yield (averaging often 1% or more above comparable Treasury securities), the government guarantee, and the monthly payments (assuming that you want monthly payments).

Many investors, attracted by the government guarantee, have failed to understand the *disadvantages* of

Ginnie Maes. First, as with any government securities, Ginnie Maes can fluctuate in market price. And Ginnie Maes carry some special complications. When you own a Ginnie Mae, monthly payments are a pass-through of mortgage payments that consist of both interest and principal, and your payments will vary, depending on the rate at which the underlying mortgage borrowers *prepay* their mortgages. It's figured that the *average* length of a Ginnie Mae certificate is 12 years, based on the *average* rate of prepayment of mortgages, but actual experience is different on each certificate, and can't be predicted ahead of time.

In particular, when interest rates are falling, homeowners often pay off old, high-rate mortgages in order to refinance with lower-rate mortgages. This happened in 1985 and 1986. Many Ginnie Mae certificates that were backed by old 12% or 13% mortgages had been selling at premium prices (i.e., prices above 100) because of the high rates they paid, and on the assumption that these high rates would continue in the future. But as the homeowners paid off their mortgages early, the life of these certificates quickly shrank, and the premiums shrank also, disappointing many certificate holders.

Ginnie Mae Unit Trusts and Mutual Funds

The minimum amount of a Ginnie Mae certificate is $25,000, which is beyond reach for many people. Brokerage firms sell "unit trusts" that permit an investor to buy a smaller share in a pool of Ginnie Mae certificates. This is workable, but be aware that your yield will be reduced by the commission paid to buy shares in the trust, and the trust shares may or may not have a ready market if you wish to sell.

Another practical approach for the average investor is to invest through the *mutual funds* that put their shareholders' money into Ginnie Maes. Shares in these funds can be bought and sold easily, and many of them are no-load (sold without commission). Expenses of the fund may reduce your yield by ¼% or 1% annually, which is a reasonable price to pay for the flexibility that a fund provides. (If the certificates are yielding

9%, your yield from the fund might be in the 8 to 8¼%
range.)

As we pointed out above, the market prices of Ginnie Mae certificates fluctuate as interest rates change, just like the prices of longer-term Treasury bonds and notes. The same price fluctuations occur in shares of the Ginnie Mae unit trusts and mutual funds. In an inflationary period, when interest rates are rising, Ginnie Maes may decline more sharply in price than regular Treasuries, depending on supply-demand factors.

Taxation of Ginnie Maes

Also, remember that the interest on a Ginnie Mae certificate is *not* exempt from state and local income taxes. If you live in a high-tax state, this can wipe out much of the yield advantage of the Ginnie Mae certificates over Treasuries.

Conclusion

How do all these pros and cons add up? If you seriously need the edge in yield that the Ginnie Maes provide, and expect to hold them for a long period, they may be a good investment for you. But if you like simplicity and flexibility, and like to be able to move easily in and out of your investments, then longer-term Treasury notes and bonds may be a more comfortable choice, despite the slightly lower yield.

15·ZERO-COUPON TREASURIES

ALTHOUGH ZERO-COUPON BONDS are a relatively recent innovation, they are already widely known. Zero-coupon bonds are so called because they pay no interest (i.e., no coupon) during the life of the bond. The interest is compounded, cumulated, and paid off in one lump sum at maturity.

The compounding effect can be staggering. For example, a 10% zero-coupon bond that you buy now for $1,420 will pay off in 20 years at $10,000.

Actually, the recent invention isn't so recent. Think back to the old U.S. Treasury War Bonds, which then became the Series E and now the Series EE savings bonds. All of these have used the zero-coupon approach, with interest cumulated and paid off at maturity. But savings bonds are not marketable, and the interest rates have usually been below those prevailing on marketable Treasuries. The new zero-coupon bonds have no such limitations.

Locking In a Compounded Rate of Return

A zero-coupon bond has the advantage of *locking in* a certain rate of return. Let's say you buy an ordinary 20-year Treasury bond with a 9% coupon. You don't intend to spend the semiannual interest payments, but to reinvest them in order to build up your capital. But what if interest rates drop? You will still be receiving interest payments at the rate of 9%, but you may be reinvesting these payments at only 6% or 7%. Your bond investment is not really compounding at 9%, but at a lower rate.

A zero-coupon bond solves that problem. It locks in the original interest rate *fully compounded*. The semiannual payments all compound at the original rate. When you buy the bond, you know exactly what your fully compounded return will be for a period that may be as long as 30 years.

Here's what it would cost *now* to buy a zero-coupon Treasury that will pay off at $1,000 in from 5 to 30 years, at various assumed interest rates:

Prices Now of $1000 of Zero Coupon Bond (All figures rounded to nearest dollar)

Years to Maturity	Interest Rate				
	6%	8%	10%	12%	14%
5 Years	$744	$676	$614	$558	$508
10	554	456	377	312	258
15	412	308	231	174	131
20	307	208	142	97	67
25	228	141	87	54	34
30	170	95	54	30	17

The Tax Problem

There are some problems with zero coupons. The main problem is that the IRS makes you pay income tax on the annual interest on the bond, even though you aren't receiving the interest in cash. Most investors don't want to pay tax on income they haven't received. (On the other hand, this can be used as a very effective forced saving device.)

But zero coupons fit very well into an IRA, Keogh or other account where there are no taxes to pay. They may also be suitable for a custodian account for a minor, depending on the minor's tax situation. (See the No Nonsense Financial Guide, *The New Tax Law and What it Means to You*.)

The Problem of Volatility

Another problem is that because of the full lock-in feature, zero-coupon bonds fluctuate much more sharply in price than regular bonds when interest rates fluctuate. If you intend to hold a bond to maturity, perhaps you aren't concerned with how the market price of the bond fluctuates in the interim. But keep in mind that if interest rates rise, and prices of existing bonds fall, zero-coupon bonds will fall much more sharply than other comparable bonds.

On the other hand, if interest rates *decline*, prices of zero-coupon bonds will *rise* more sharply than other bonds. Moreover, with zero-coupon Treasuries, there's no call feature to limit such a price rise. So if interest rates are high and bond prices are down to levels that you feel are bargains, zero coupons will give you a bigger upward swing and more profit if you are right— and more loss if you are wrong.

How Treasuries Got Zeroed

When zero coupons began to come into fashion in the early 1980s, investment firms took the lead in converting ordinary Treasury bonds into zero-coupon certificates with memorable names—such as Certificates of Accrual on Treasury Securities (CATS) and Treasury Investment Growth Receipts (TIGRs). Beginning in early 1985, the Treasury got into the game itself by offering STRIPS—which, in case you hadn't guessed, are Separate Trading of Registered Interest and Principal of Securities.

All of these are actively traded, and the leading brokerage firms deal in various types. If you think that zero coupons might suit you—especially for an IRA or the other purposes mentioned above—shop around and use a firm that deals in the quantities and maturities you want.

Brokers' commissions on zeros are usually a higher percentage of the purchase price than with regular bonds. Do enough shopping to make sure that the commissions you will be charged by a particular broker are competitive. And make sure that there is an active trading market in the breed and maturity of zeros you intend to buy, in case you want to sell them later on.

16· ANOTHER ROAD: MUTUAL FUNDS AND UNIT TRUSTS

ONE PROBLEM WITH TREASURIES is that they come in big units. The smallest unit, as we've said, is $10,000 for bills, and $5,000 for shorter-term notes. The bonds and longer-term notes come in denominations of $1,000; but if you buy or sell a single $1,000 bond in the market, the minimum broker's commission of $25 or $35 is large on a percentage basis.

An easy way around this problem is to invest in Treasuries through a *mutual fund*. A mutual fund is a way of pooling the money of many investors so that it can be managed efficiently and economically as a single large unit. Mutual funds bring many types of investments within the reach of even the smallest investor, for whom the costs of direct investing are often out of proportion to the amount involved. (For more information, see the No Nonsense Financial Guide, *Understanding Mutual Funds*.)

The "Government-Only" Money Market Funds

The best-known type of mutual fund is probably the *money market fund*, where the fund's money is invested for maximum safety only in the shortest-term income-producing investments. (For more information, see the No Nonsense Financial Guide, *Understanding Money Market Funds*.)

While the general money market funds have had a completely safe record for investors, the fund industry has gone a step farther by creating a group of money market funds that invest *only* in U.S. government secu-

54

rities. When you buy shares in one of these funds, you own a proportionate interest in a pool of Treasury bills and other short-term government securities.

With investments restricted in this way, and with the funds regulated closely by the Securities and Exchange Commission, the safety you enjoy by owning shares in these funds is only a shade less than if you owned Treasury bills directly. The safety factor is, in our opinion, high enough for anyone.

Some representative funds of this type are listed in Appendix B. The funds have several advantages. Starting minimums may be as little as $1,000 or even $500. You can invest and withdraw relatively small amounts easily, with no commissions whatsoever. You can have the income paid to you in cash or reinvested. You can write checks on your fund account, with certain restrictions, and can enjoy other conveniences.

Some Disadvantages

Of course, you pay a certain price for these advantages. The expenses of running the fund are subtracted from your yield. The larger, more efficient funds may have annual expenses of about ¾ of 1% of assets. Some of this is offset by the ability of the funds to trade effectively in large quantities with very low commissions. Still, in a government-only money market fund, you will probably earn about ½ of 1% *less* on your money than you would by investing in Treasury bills directly.

The State and Local Tax Problem

There's another possible disadvantage, depending on where you live. In Chapter 13, we pointed out that the interest paid on Treasury securities is exempt from state and local income tax. But if you own shares in a government securities *fund*—either a government-only money market fund, or one of the longer-term government funds discussed below—the fund dividends are exempt from tax in some states, but not in all.

The funds argue that their dividend payments to

shareholders should be exempt from state and local income taxes, since the payments represent a pass-through of interest on government securities. But several states take the position that the income loses this exemption when it passes through the fund.

The trend, both through court cases and through legislation, seems to be in favor of the government-only funds and their shareholders. But as of early 1987, there were about 20 states that continued to tax government-fund dividends. And even in the "tax-free" states, there may be problems depending on a fund's portfolio—for example, a few states won't allow the exemption if most of the fund's income comes from Ginnie Maes. So it's advisable to check the problem with your tax attorney, accountant, or with the tax authorities in your state.

Longer-term Funds

There are also a number of mutual funds that invest in intermediate-term and longer-term government securities. Just as the government-only money market funds are an alternative to owning Treasury bills, so these longer-term funds are an alternative to owning Treasury notes and/or bonds directly.

A list of certain of the larger funds of this type is given in Appendix C. You need to read the prospectus and latest reports of each fund to know what types of government securities it holds, and what range of maturities is included in its portfolio. The policy varies from fund to fund, and is usually clearly stated.

In buying any fund that holds longer-term securities, you need to exercise an extra degree of care. You want to know not only that the fund has achieved a reasonable yield, but also that the managers have handled the fund well in relation to price swings in the market. Look at the 5-year record of the fund to see if any capital gains have been earned for shareholders, or if the managers have succeeded in building up the value ("net asset value per share") of the shares. Compare at least a few of these funds before you buy. (For more information on choosing mutual funds, see the

No Nonsense Financial Guide, *Understanding Mutual Funds.)*

Certain of the longer-term government-only funds actually invest part or even all of their portfolios in Ginnie Mae mortgage certificates. As we pointed out in Chapter 14; these are very different securities from Treasury bonds and notes; they may produce higher yields, but they also add significant elements of uncertainty to the portfolio.

All the longer-term funds are different in significant respects from the money market funds. In the longer-term funds, prices of the shares can fluctuate, and may sometimes swing widely in price in response to swings in the bond market. Moreover, there usually are no check-writing privileges, and redemption (sale) of shares is usually not as simple as with a money market fund.

There are other areas where the two types of funds are similar. With the longer-term funds, as with the money market funds, yields are usually from ½ of 1% to 1% below what you might earn by owning comparable Treasuries directly. And the possible lack of exemption from state income taxes is the same as with the money market funds.

On the other hand, minimum required investments in the longer-term funds are usually lower (often as low as $500), and you have a high degree of flexibility in terms of being able to deposit and withdraw relatively small amounts of money. While some of these funds may be sold with a commission (*load*), others are sold and redeemed without commission (on a *no-load* basis), so that you can move in and out flexibly with no transaction cost whatsoever.

Finally, a good management may save you money, or perhaps make profits for you, by making good judgments as to which Treasury issues to buy, when to buy them, and when to sell them. And, just as with the money market funds, the fund will save relatively on transaction costs because of the large scale on which it buys and sells. So a no-load fund of this type, with a good management and a good record, can be very attractive to the average investor.

Unit Trusts

Unit trusts are a different type of investment pool. In a mutual fund, professional managers are responsible for continuous management of the fund's securities (its *portfolio*), buying the most attractive securities when the fund has cash available, and selling securities that appear, for one reason or another, to have become less attractive. A unit trust, on the other hand, starts out with a specific assortment of securities that usually remain unchanged for the life of the trust, except as they may mature and be paid off.

Shares in the trust are usually offered with a commission. The size of the commission has to be viewed in relation to the length of the trust. If you divide the commission by the number of years you expect to own the trust shares, you can see how much per year it will subtract from your yield. A deduction of between ½ of 1% and 1% annually is not unreasonable if the trust permits you to make a type of investment that would otherwise be impractical for you.

The trust form permits a pass-through of income that is even more direct than with a mutual fund. For example, unit trusts are commonly used as a way of packaging Ginnie Mae certificates so that participations are available in smaller units than the usual $25,000 minimum on the certificates. The trust form permits a direct pass-through of the monthly payments, including both interest and principal. In contrast, mutual funds that hold Ginnie Mae certificates usually pass through the interest component of the monthly payments, but not the principal, which is reinvested by the fund.

17·FLOWER BONDS

FLOWER BONDS ARE CERTAIN TREASURY bonds, issued before 1972, which are accepted by the government at *face value* in payment of federal estate taxes.

The bonds, having been issued many years ago, all carry low coupons (low stated interest rates), and trade in the market at a discount from par. So the bonds can be bought at a discount by taxpayers in anticipation of death, and then, after death, can be used at full face value by the executors of the estate in payment of taxes. Hence the nickname, "flower bonds." Here is a list of the issues that qualify:

Flower Bonds

Coupon	Maturity	Approx. Price	Face Value
3½%	Feb. 15, 1990	$940	$1000
4¼	Aug. 15, 1992-87	$940	$1000
4	Feb. 15, 1993–88	$940	$1000
4⅛	May 15, 1994–89	$940	$1000
3	Feb. 15, 1995	$940	$1000
3½	Nov. 15, 1998	$940	$1000

Where two dates are shown, the bonds are callable beginning in the earlier year. But the Treasury would have no reason to redeem bonds early on which it pays such low interest rates.

There are a few problems, and it's wise to consult a tax attorney or accountant before making use of flower bonds. First, because of the special estate tax advantage, the bonds sell at relatively higher prices and substantially lower yields than other Treasury bonds. So if bought long before death, the loss of yield can offset the tax advantage.

Second, the tax advantage applies only if the bonds are owned by the decedent at the time of death, and it's important that the bonds be bought sufficiently before death so that there can be no dispute. Death-bed purchases engineered by relatives are likely to be challenged by the IRS.

Third, in community property states, when one of two spouses dies, only half the bonds purchased may be permitted to be applied to estate tax payments. As we said—before using these bonds, see your tax attorney or accountant.

18·SAVINGS BONDS

THROUGHOUT THIS BOOK WE have talked about *marketable* U.S. government securities—the securities that trade in billions of dollars every day and that are a cornerstone of the investment markets.

But many Americans are much more familiar with a completely different type of security—the U.S. Treasury savings bonds that sell for amounts as low as $25 and that are bought by a multitude of small investors, often through payroll savings plans.

Good Buy or Bad Buy?

Years ago, savings bonds paid interest rates far below those on marketable U.S. Treasuries, and the bonds were criticized as short-changing the small investor. But over the years, the Treasury has raised the rates, and now the rates on the basic Series EE bonds are directly linked to those on marketable Treasuries.

The bonds come in denominations (face value) of from $50 to $10,000, and you buy them for one-half of face value. So you pay $25 for a $50 bond, or $500 for a $1,000 bond, and so on. But the face value isn't really important, since the time the bond takes to reach face value depends on the interest rate you earn, and the interest rate generally varies. Also, there's no requirement that you hold the bond until it reaches face value.

In fact, you can cash Series EE bonds in at any time. *But* you only receive a favorable interest rate if the bonds are held for five years or more. For bonds held more than five years, the rate you receive is the *higher* of (a) 85% of the average rate on 5-year Treasuries prevailing during the period (based on a calculation made by the Treasury every six months), and (b) a guaranteed minimum.

For several years, the guaranteed minimum was

7½%. In late 1986, it was reduced to 6% for all new EE bond purchases. Watch for possible further changes in the minimum; and note that while you can't earn *less* than the minimum on EE bonds held more than five years, you can easily earn *more* if market rates are high. A bond that earns the 6% minimum will reach face value (double your cost) in 12 years. Bonds cashed in before 5 years are credited with interest at lower rates.

Buying Series EE Bonds

As we said, purchase prices on the EE bonds range from $25 to $5,000; the maximum that can be invested by an individual in any one year is $15,000. Bonds can be registered in the name of (a) an individual, (b) co-owners (in which case either co-owner may cash the bond), or (c) an individual and a beneficiary. They can also be registered in the names of fiduciaries and organizations.

Savings bonds *cannot* be transferred, sold, or used as collateral for a loan.

The Original Zero Coupons

As we said in an earlier chapter, U.S. savings bonds were perhaps the original zero-coupon issues. The EE bonds follow this pattern, with interest compounded semiannually, cumulated, and paid out only when the bonds are cashed in.

But there's an advantage over ordinary zero-coupon issues. While you have the option of paying income tax on the interest every year, you aren't *required* to pay it until the bonds are cashed in, and most investors defer the tax payment until then.

There's a way of deferring the tax even beyond maturity. You can exchange your Series EE bonds for Series HH bonds, which don't cumulate interest but pay it out semiannually at the annual rate of 7.5%. You pay current taxes on this 7.5% interest, but you continue to defer the income tax you owed on your EE bonds until the HH bonds are finally disposed of. The HH bonds have a maturity of 10 years and come in minimum denominations of $500.

As with marketable Treasuries, the interest on both EE and HH bonds is subject to federal income tax but *not* to state and local income taxes. The bonds *are* subject to estate, gift, and inheritance taxes.

Saving For Minors

Because of the tax deferral, Series EE bonds can be one of the most effective ways of saving for a child's education. Under the Tax Reform Act of 1986, unearned income of a child under age 14, to the extent that it exceeds $1,000 per year, is taxed at the parents' tax rate rather than the child's. But once the child reaches age 14, unearned income is taxed at the child's rate. (For more detailed information, see the No Nonsense Financial Guide, *The New Tax Law and What It Means to You.*)

So, for example, Series EE bonds can be bought in the name of a child (or in the name of an adult as custodian for a child under the Uniform Gifts to Minors Act), and the bonds can later be redeemed when the child is 18 and about to enter college. Tax on the interest would be deferred until the time of redemption, and the tax would then be at the child's (presumably lower) tax bracket.

A Tax Gimmick

There's a different tax approach worth considering if the annual income earned on a child's EE bonds, plus any other income the child has, is *not* high enough to subject the child to income tax.

Even if the child has no other income, the lump-sum interest received at maturity might be enough to trigger an income tax payment. If this appears likely, then instead of waiting, you declare the interest annually as you go along.

In the first year, a tax return is filed in the name of the child, declaring that year's interest—which presumably won't be large enough for any tax to be due. This establishes the intent to declare the interest annually. (Keep a copy of the tax return!) In succeeding years, it's assumed that you are regarding each year's interest as taxable to the child, but a tax return doesn't actually have to be filed for the child unless the child has enough income so that a tax actually is due.

At maturity, there's no tax to pay (except possibly on the final year's interest). The money is there, free and clear—ready for college tuition, or whatever other purpose it was intended for.

Yes, a Good Buy

Under current rules, we would sum up by saying that savings bonds (EE bonds) are a better buy than most people realize—and for the small investor, a very good savings device.

First, the small denominations can be a great convenience. Second, the bonds can be an excellent forced saving device, either through payroll deduction or otherwise. Third, the interest rate is now close to that on marketable Treasuries—and, if interest rates should fall sharply in coming years, you have the 6% floor to fall back on. Fourth, you can defer income tax on the interest until the bonds are cashed. Fifth, you enjoy the exemption from state and local income taxes. Sixth, the bonds are bought and redeemed without commission. Finally, the bonds can always be redeemed at a prefixed value, and are not subject to market fluctuations.

It's not a bad list. Think it over, and consider whether savings bonds may meet any of your needs.

Older Savings Bonds

Many people still hold old Series E and Series H bonds issued anywhere from 1941 to 1980. Most of these are continuing to earn interest, with the exception of some of the earliest bonds in both series.

If you own any such bonds, especially those that have passed their original maturity dates, make sure you know the rules and for how long they will continue to earn interest. If you have bonds that are no longer earning interest, they should of course be cashed in. Old Series E bonds can be exchanged into new Series HH bonds until one year after final maturity. For full information, ask at your local bank or see your nearest Federal Reserve bank or branch.

PART V

YOUR INVESTMENT STRATEGY

19. YOUR INVESTMENT OBJECTIVES

IN THIS BOOK WE have discussed the many advantages of U.S. Treasury securities. We have pointed out that Treasuries give you:

- The highest degree of safety
- High liquidity
- Relatively high yields
- Interest from day of purchase to day of sale
- Low commissions or no commissions
- Borrowing power
- Exemption from state and local income taxes

Still, you have to view Treasuries as against alternative investments, and you have to view them in relation to your own investment objectives.

Your investment goals probably represent some combination of these three objectives:

- Safety and preservation of your principal
- Income on your investments
- Growth of your investments

There is always some degree of trade-off among these objectives. If you aim for growth, you are bound to give up a certain amount of safety. Even if you push for higher income, you will usually have to give up some safety.

The Inflation Problem

The choices are made more difficult because of the existence of inflation. Because the value of each of your dollars shrinks every year, preserving your capital in terms of dollars isn't enough. You need to preserve the *purchasing power* or *real value* of your investments by making your dollars grow at least enough to offset the effects of inflation.

The inflation rate has gone through wide swings in recent years. It reached double-digit territory (above 10%) in 1979 and 1980, then dropped sharply to below 4% in the 1983–86 period. Inflation is hard to predict, especially since it depends heavily on political decisions. But the wisest course in planning your investments is to assume that inflation is still a substantial problem. The underlying causes—particularly the federal budget deficit—are still very much with us. It's hard to imagine inflation staying down at the 2% to 3% level of the 1950s and 1960s.

Growth vs. Income Investments

Some investments help you adjust to inflation, while others don't. Many people deal with the inflation problem by choosing *growth* investments—by investing in a company or property that is expected to grow in value over time. But it's also possible to make your capital grow through an *income* investment, if the income is substantial and if you plow part or all of it back to add to the value of your capital. For example, we saw in Chapter 15 how effectively zero-coupon bonds can make your money grow if bought at a time when bond yields are high.

This approach won't give you the spectacular results that people sometimes achieve in true growth investments. But it can give you more certainty of results each year, more stability, and less price fluctuation. If you want to keep your risks to a minimum, it's a workable way to proceed.

As we've pointed out earlier, U.S. government securities are a better investment than they used to be. Years ago, when yields on Treasuries were very low, it was hard to recommend them except for great safety and limited income. Now the income is higher, and there's a definite potential for converting that income into long-term growth.

20·TREASURY BILLS AS AN INVESTMENT

PROFESSIONAL INVESTORS USE TREASURY bills constantly as a short-term investment—a way of temporarily investing cash that isn't being used for longer-term investments, and getting a reasonable return in the meanwhile.

If you deal in large amounts, you too can use bills as a temporary investment. Or, if you are dealing with fewer dollars, you may choose a government-only money market fund as one of your alternatives.

But what about T-bills as a longer-term investment? Many people buy bills that way. Some people are quite happy having a substantial part of their investment capital invested in bills, perhaps buying them commission-free through the Treasury or a Federal Reserve bank and having them automatically renewed at each maturity.

Protection against Inflation

You won't make a killing owning Treasury bills, but you won't lose money either. Interestingly enough, as long as you keep plowing back your interest, the bills will give you some protection against inflation. Why? Because interest rates generally rise when inflation is high, and decline when inflation is low. So when inflation heats up, it's likely that the rates on T-bills will rise correspondingly. In 1981, T-bill yields averaged 14% and actually, at one point, reached 16%.

So the interest you earn on your T-bills each year will probably be enough to make up for that year's inflation, and perhaps a little more. The *real* value of your investment—its *purchasing power*—will probably grow moderately or at least hold even, as long as you are plowing the interest back.

A government-only money market fund will probably achieve the same goal for you, despite the slightly lower yield. For the investor with limited capital who wants both absolute safety and immediate access to his or her money, these funds are generally an attractive choice.

21·TREASURY BONDS: PROFITS AND PERILS

As you go from shorter-term Treasuries to longer-term, the problems from an investment viewpoint become more complex.

Shorter-term Treasury notes (2 to 4 years) are often used as an alternative to bills, and carry many of the same qualities. Market prices of the notes fluctuate in response to changes in interest rates, but the fluctuations are usually not too sharp, since the notes will be paid off at face value in a relatively short time. When you can get a much better yield by buying, say, a 2-year note rather than a 6-month bill, it may be worth taking this modest price risk.

Longer Maturities, Higher Risks

Longer-term bonds used to be regarded as stable, secure, conservative investments. But the uncertainties of inflation and interest rates have changed the bond investment scene drastically.

When interest rates rise, prices of old bonds decline. It's easy to see why. If you buy a long-term Treasury bond paying 10%, and interest rates then rise to 14%, investors who can now buy 14% bonds certainly will not pay full value in the market for your 10% bond. So the market price of your bond will decline according to a mathematical formula. If your bond is a Treasury, you still know without a doubt that it will be paid off in full at maturity. Nevertheless, if you want to sell it now in the market, you will take a loss.

Exactly this kind of situation prevailed in the bond market for many long, difficult years from the mid-1960s to 1981. As inflation heated up and interest rates rose, bond prices slid painfully downward. At the worst, in 1981, some Treasury bonds were selling at around 60 cents on the dollar.

The following chart shows Treasury bond interest rates from 1960 to 1986:

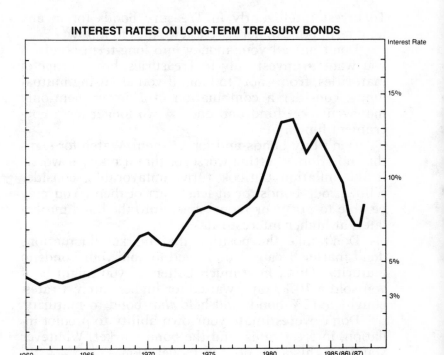

INTEREST RATES ON LONG-TERM TREASURY BONDS

The Need for Alertness

Does this mean that you shouldn't invest in long-term bonds? No, but it means that you should recognize the risks and learn the lessons. Bonds are investments that do *not* adjust flexibly to inflation—quite the opposite. They are usually a good holding when inflation and interest rates are falling, a poor holding when inflation and interest rates are heating up.

The good times can be very good. We've just referred to the long decline in bond prices that climaxed in 1981. But remember that earlier in this book, we looked at some of the bonds that the Treasury sold at rates of up to 15% when the bond market was at its worst. By 1985, investors in those bonds had profits in some cases running above 30%.

Some Rules

To invest intelligently in Treasury bonds (or in any long-term bonds), here are a few rules to follow:

Don't put all your money into long-term bonds. If you want to invest only in Treasuries, buy a range of maturities, from short to long. If you are using mutual funds, consider a combination of a government-only money market fund and one or two longer-term government funds.

Don't buy bonds and forget them. Watch for signs that inflation is getting worse, or that it may get worse. If the inflation outlook turns unfavorable, consider selling your bonds, or at least part of them. You may be able to put your money back into the bond market later, at higher interest rates.

Don't take the position that market fluctuations don't matter because you intend to hold your bonds to maturity. Think how much better off you might be if you sold a 10% bond, waited for higher interest rates, bought a 12% bond, and held *that* bond to maturity.

Don't overestimate your own ability to predict inflation, interest rates, and the bond market. Whatever you do in this area, do it in moderation.

Don't be swayed too much by experts who tell you that *they* can predict inflation, interest rates, and the bond market. The best economists in the world have often had dismal records in this area.

When you do think that bonds are a good buy, consider buying bonds of about 10-year maturities rather than the very long issues. In that way you will limit your potential for profit, but also your potential for loss. And you don't usually gain significantly in yield by going out beyond 10 years.

Consider the merits of the mutual funds investing in government securities that have good performance records. Their managers probably can't predict the bond market perfectly either, but they have shown that they know how to limit their risks.

When Are Bonds a Good Buy?

Is there any magical formula to use in determining when bonds are a good investment?

Not really. Markets are too difficult to predict or summarize. Obviously, if you know how to sense when interest rates are at a peak, and bond prices at a low, those are good times to buy. Those are usually also the times when everyone tells you that bonds are certainly headed lower and that you should avoid them.

But don't let the problems drive you away. Because bond buyers have become skeptical, bonds tend to be issued today with relatively generous yields, and there have been many good buying opportunities.

Years ago, it was considered normal for bonds to be issued carrying interest rates that were perhaps 3% above the rate of inflation. As the professionals like to put it, the *real rate of return* was about 3%. In early 1985, when the inflation rate was down to around 4% or less, Treasuries were available at yields of 11% to 12%, for a real rate of return of 7% to 8%. Of course, this reflected investors' fears that the rate of inflation would soon turn up again. But inflation did not turn up again—at least, not in the short run. In 1986, yields on long-term Treasuries dropped below 8% for a time, and investors who had been wise enough to buy bonds in 1985 saw their bonds rise very nicely in price.

The moral: whenever the outlook is for lower inflation and interest rates, longer-term Treasuries may be a good buy. And the higher the real rate of return when you buy, the greater your margin of protection against error. But, as we've said before, even the most expert forecasts often go wrong. So, after you buy—stay alert.

22·TREASURIES AND BEYOND

WE STARTED THIS BOOK by saying that U.S. government securities are regarded as the safest investments in the world. That's true. But we've ended the book by showing that there are risks even in U.S. Treasuries.

This isn't meant as a paradox. Investing is a complicated art, with no easy answers. You have to be alert to many possibilities, alert to change, alert to the hidden risks that often exist in what may appear to be the safest investments.

To get the most out of your government securities investments, you have to be alert to inflation, interest rates, and changes in the tax rules. And you have to learn to define your own investment objectives clearly.

To those investors who hesitate to venture beyond government securities to other types of investments, this carries a useful message. If you have learned to watch your investments in governments intelligently, then you have also learned many of the lessons you need in order to look intelligently at other investments.

The same alertness can make you a good investor in other areas. If you are in a high tax bracket, you can consider the tax advantages of municipal bonds. If you need every bit of extra yield, you can consider corporate bonds in addition to Treasuries. If you want to see your money grow faster over the long term, you can explore the possibilities of common stocks, where a moderate additional risk can often bring major monetary rewards. In all these areas, you can learn to select high-quality mutual funds, where professional managers relieve you of the burden of choosing and managing individual securities.

So while Treasuries may always be a cornerstone of your investment portfolio, they can also be a stepping stone into the wider world of even more fascinating and sometimes more profitable investments. We hope this book will encourage you to make the most of your investments and to explore more fully both U.S. Treasuries and that wider world.

GLOSSARY

Accrued Interest See Chapter 9.

Asked Price (or Asking Price) The price at which a dealer offers to sell a security.

Asset Any property owned.

Auction In Treasury securities, the procedure by which new Treasury issues are sold to those bidders who offer to buy at the highest prices (that is, at the lowest effective yields).

Basis Point 1/100 of 1% (.01%).

Bearer Bond See Bearer Security and Coupon Bond.

Bearer Security A security that is not registered in anyone's name, but belongs to whoever has physical possession of it.

Bid Price The price at which a dealer offers to buy a security.

Bill See Treasury Bill.

Bond A long-term debt security issued by a government or corporation promising repayment of a given amount by a given date, plus interest.

Book-entry System A system where ownership of securities is recorded on a central registry without issuance of physical certificates. The Federal Reserve maintains such a system for U.S. Government securities.

Broker See Brokerage Firm. Also, specifically, an individual or firm that acts as agent, for a commission, in buying or selling securities or other property for others.

Broker-Dealer See Brokerage Firm.

Brokerage Firm A term including several types of firms in the securities business that usually do business with the public.

Call A bond is called when all or part of an issue is redeemed before maturity. See Chapter 10.

Callable A callable bond is one that may be redeemed by the issuer under certain conditions prior to maturity.

Capital Wealth invested or available for investment.

Capital Gain The profit from sale of a security or other asset at a price above its cost.

CATS Certificates of Accrual on Treasury Securities—one of the brokerage firm brand names for zero-coupon Treasury bonds.

CD (Certificate of Deposit) A "time deposit" in a bank, maturing on a specific date and traditionally evidenced by a certificate.

Certificate The piece of paper (usually engraved) evidencing ownership of a security.

Commission The fee paid to a broker for buying or selling securities or other property.

Compound Interest Interest calculated both on the principal of an investment and on the accumulated interest previously credited.

Coupon The stated rate of interest on a bond. On a bearer bond, the coupons are the stubs that are clipped and presented to receive interest.

Coupon Bond A bond in bearer form with coupons attached that are periodically clipped and presented to receive interest.

Current Yield Annual income paid on a bond or other investment, expressed as a percentage of the current market price.

Dealer A person or firm in the business of buying and selling securities. Specifically, a dealer acts as principal rather than agent, buying and selling for his/her own account.

Debt Security A security representing a promise by the issuer to repay a certain amount by a given date, plus interest.

Face Value The face value or principal amount of a bond is the amount the issuer promises to repay at maturity.

FDIC (Federal Deposit Insurance Corp.) The federal agency that insures deposits at member banks (up to $100,000).

Federal Reserve System The central bank of the United States, composed of twelve regional Federal Reserve banks and headed by the Board of Governors.

Fixed-Income Security A security promising a specified rate of payment of interest or dividends.

Flower Bonds See Chapter 17.

FNMA The Federal National Mortgage Association, known as Fannie Mae—a quasi-governmental agency, now publicly owned, that purchases mortgages from the original mortgage lenders.

FSLIC (Federal Savings and Loan Insurance Corp.) The federal agency that insures deposits at member savings and loan associations (up to $100,000).

GNMA The Government National Mortgage Association, known as Ginnie Mae—a quasi-governmental agency, carrying the full faith and credit of the U.S. government, that purchases mortgages from the original mortgage lenders.

Interest Rate The rate of payment on a debt obligation, usually stated as a percentage of cost or face value.

Liquid Investment An investment that can be converted easily into cash, without penalty.

Load The sales charge or commission charged on purchase of some mutual funds.

Margin Buying a security on margin means that part of the purchase price is borrowed from a broker. The margin is the amount the customer puts up.

Maturity The maturity date is the date when a debt obligation is due to be repaid.

Money Fund A money market fund.

Money Market A phrase to describe the tremendous informal network through which hundreds of billions of dollars are regularly lent on a short-term basis among governments, banks, corporations and other institutions.

Money Market Fund A mutual fund that aims at maximum safety, liquidity, and a constant price for its shares. Its assets are invested to earn current market interest rates on the safest, short-term, highly liquid investments.

Mutual Fund An open-end investment company that pools the money of many investors to provide them with professional management, diversification and other advantages.

Negotiable Refers to a security whose ownership is easily transferable from one person to another.

No-load Fund A mutual fund that sells its shares at net asset value, without any commission.

Note See Treasury Note.

Par In bonds, a price of 100, which stands for 100% of face value (that is, a price of $1,000 for a $1,000 bond).

Portfolio The total list of securities owned by an investor.

Principal The capital or main body of an investment, as distinguished from the income earned on it. Also, a dealer or other individual buying or selling for his own account.

Principal Amount See Face Value.

Quotation, Quote A report of the current bid and asked prices on a security.

Redemption In bonds, the repayment of the bond principal amount by the issuer.

Savings Bonds See Chapter 18.

Security General term meaning stocks, bonds and other investment instruments.

SIPC (Securities Investor Protection Corp.) A nonprofit organization to which most brokerage firms belong and which insures accounts of their customers up to $500,000.

Street Name Securities registered in the name of a brokerage firm rather than in the name of the customer are said to be held in street name.

STRIPS Separate Trading of Registered Interest and Principal of Securities—the U.S. Treasury's own variety of zero-coupon Treasury bonds.

T-bill See Treasury Bill.

TIGRs Treasury Investment Growth Receipts—one of the brokerage firm brand names for zero-coupon Treasury bonds.

Treasuries U.S. Treasury securities.

Treasury Bill A short-term debt security of the U.S. Treasury, issued with a maturity of 3, 6 or 12 months and sold on a discounted basis.

Treasury Bond A U.S. Treasury debt security with an original maturity of more than 10 years from the date of issuance.

Treasury Note A U.S. Treasury debt security with an original maturity of from 1 to 10 years from the date of issuance.

Unit Trust See Chapter 16.

Yield The return on an investment. In securities, the interest or dividends received, usually expressed as an annual percentage of either the current market value or the cost of the investment.

Yield to Maturity See Chapter 7.

Zero-Coupon Bond See Chapter 15.

APPENDIX A

U.S. Treasury and Federal Reserve Banks

U.S. Treasury Department (general information)	Bureau of the Public Debt Securities Transactions Branch Main Treasury Bldg., Room 2134 Washington, DC 20226 (202) 566-2604
Board of Governors Federal Reserve System	20th and Constitution Ave., N.W. Washington, DC 20551 (202) 452-3000

Federal Reserve Banks and Branches

Bank of Boston	600 Atlantic Ave. Boston, MA 02106 (617) 973-3800
Bank of New York	33 Liberty St. (Federal Reserve P.O. Station) New York, NY 10045 (212) 791-5823
Buffalo Branch	160 Delaware Ave. (P.O. Box 961) Buffalo, NY 14240 (716) 849-5046
Bank of Philadelphia	100 N. Sixth St. (P.O. Box 90) Philadelphia, PA 19105 (215) 574-6580
Bank of Cleveland	1455 E. Sixth St. (P.O. Box 6387) Cleveland, OH 44101 (216) 579-2490
Cincinnati Branch	150 E. Fourth St. (P.O. Box 999) Cincinnati, OH 45201 (513) 721-4787
Pittsburgh Branch	717 Grant St. (P.O. Box 867) Pittsburgh, PA 15230 (412) 261-7864

Bank of Richmond	701 E. Byrd St. (P.O. Box 27622) Richmond, VA 23261 (804) 643-1250
Baltimore Branch	502 S. Sharp St. (P.O. Box 1378) Baltimore, MD 21203 (301) 576-3300
Charlotte Branch	401 S. Tryon St. (P.O. Box 30248) Charlotte, NC 28230 (704) 373-0200
Bank of Atlanta	104 Marietta St. N.W. (P.O. Box 1731) Atlanta, GA 30301 (404) 586-8657
Birmingham Branch	1801 Fifth Ave., North (P.O. Box 10447) Birmingham, AL 35202 (205) 252-3141
Jacksonville Branch	515 Julia St. Jacksonville, FL 32231 (904) 354-8211
Miami Branch	3770 S.W. Eighth St. Coral Gables, FL 33134 (P.O. Box 847, Miami, FL 33152) (305) 591-2065
Nashville Branch	301 Eighth Ave., North Nashville, TN 37203 (615) 259-4006
New Orleans Branch	525 St. Charles Ave. (P.O. Box 61630) New Orleans, LA 70161 (504) 586-1505
Bank of Chicago	230 S. LaSalle St. (P.O. Box 834) Chicago, IL 60690 (312) 786-1110
Detroit Branch	160 Fort St., West (P.O. Box 1059) Detroit, MI 48231 (313) 961-6880
Bank of St. Louis	411 Locust St. (P.O. Box 442) St. Louis, MO 63166 (314) 444-8444
Little Rock Branch	325 W. Capitol Ave. (P.O. Box 1261) Little Rock, AR 72203 (501) 372-5451

83

Louisville Branch	410 S. Fifth St. (P.O. Box 899) Louisville, KY 40201 (502) 568-9200
Memphis Branch	200 N. Main St. (P.O. Box 407) Memphis, TN 38101 (901) 523-7171
Bank of Minneapolis	250 Marquette Ave. Minneapolis, MN 55480 (612) 340-2051
Helena Branch	400 N. Park Ave. Helena, MT 59601 (406) 442-3860
Bank of Kansas City	925 Grand Ave. (Federal Reserve Station) Kansas City, MO 64198 (816) 881-2783
Denver Branch	1020 16th St. (P.O. Box 5228, Terminal Annex) Denver, CO 80217 (303) 292-4020
Oklahoma City Branch	226 N.W. Third St. (P.O. Box 25129) Oklahoma City, OK 73125 (405) 235-1721
Omaha Branch	102 S. 17th St. Omaha, NE 68102 (402) 341-3610
Bank of Dallas	400 S. Akard St. (Station K) Dallas, TX 75222 (214) 651-6177
El Paso Branch	301 E. Main St. (P.O. Box 100) El Paso, TX 79999 (915) 544-4730
Houston Branch	1701 San Jacinto St. (P.O. Box 2578) Houston, TX 77001 (713) 659-4433
San Antonio Branch	126 E. Nueva St. (P.O. Box 1471) San Antonio, TX 78295 (512) 224-2141
Bank of San Francisco	400 Sansome St. (P.O. Box 7702) San Francisco, CA 94120 (415) 392-6639

84

Los Angeles Branch	409 W. Olympic Blvd.
	(P.O. Box 2077, Terminal Annex)
	Los Angeles, CA 90051
	(213) 683-8563
Portland Branch	915 S.W. Stark St.
	(P.O. Box 3436)
	Portland, OR 97208
	(503) 221-5931
Salt Lake City Branch	120 S. State St.
	(P.O. Box 30780)
	Salt Lake City, UT 84127
	(801) 355-3131
Seattle Branch	1015 Second Ave.
	(P.O. Box 3567)
	Seattle, WA 98124
	(206) 442-1650

APPENDIX B

Selected Larger Money Market Funds Investing in U.S. Government Securities Only

Name	Minimum Initial Investment/ Subsequent Investment	Toll-free Telephone Number
Alliance Government Reserves, Inc.	$250/50	(800) 221-5672
Alex. Brown Cash Reserve—Govt. Series	$1000/100	(800) 558-4069
Capital Preservation Fund	$1000/100	(800) 4-SAFETY
Capital Preservation Fund II	$1000/100	(800) 4-SAFETY
Cardinal Government Securities Trust	$1000/100	(800) 848-7734
Carnegie Government Securities Trust	$1000/250	(800) 321-2322

Cash Equivalent Fund, Inc.— Government Securities Portfolio	$1000/100	(800) 621-1048
DBL Cash Fund, Inc.—Government Securities Portfolio	$1000/100	(800) 272-2700
Dean Witter/Sears U.S. Government Money Market Trust	$1000/50	(800) 233-3362
Dreyfus Money Market Instruments Inc.—Government Securities Series	$2500/100	(800) 645-6561
Fidelity U.S. Government Reserves	$1000/250	(800) 544-6666
First Variable Rate Fund for Government Income, Inc.	$2000/250	(800) 368-2748
Franklin Federal Money Fund	$500/25	(800) 632-2350
Fund for Government Investors, Inc.	$2500/none	(800) 343-3355
Government Investors Trust	$1000/none	(800) 336-3063
Hilliard Lyons Government Fund, Inc.	$3000/500	(800) 626-2023
Kemper Government Money Market Fund, Inc.	$1000/100	(800) 621-1048
Lehman Government Fund, Inc.	$1000/100	(800) 221-5350
Midwest Income Trust—Short Term Government Fund	$1000/50	(800) 543-8721
T. Rowe Price U.S. Treasury Money Fund, Inc.	$1000/100	(800) 638-5660
Prudential-Bache Govt. Securities—Money Market Series	$1000/100	(800) 642-3503
The Reserve Fund Inc.— Government Portfolio	$1000/none	(800) 223-5547
Scudder Government Money Fund	$1000/none	(800) 225-2470
Vanguard Money Market Trust— Federal Portfolio	$1000/100	(800) 662-2739

APPENDIX C

Selected Larger Mutual Funds Investing in U.S. Government Securities Only

(No-load and Low-load)

Name	Minimum Initial Investment	Maximum Sales Charge (%)	Telephone Number
Fidelity Govt. Securities	1,000	0	(800) 544-6666
Midwest Income Trust—Intermediate Term Govt.	1,000	2.0	(800) 543-8721
Prudential-Bache Govt. Securities—Intermediate Term	1,000	0	(800) 872-7787
Twentieth Century U.S. Govts.	No Min.	0	(800) 345-2021
United Govt. Securities	500	4.0	(816) 283-4000
Value Line U.S. Govt. Securities	1,000	0	(800) 223-0818
GNMA FUNDS			
Dreyfus GNMA Fund	2,500	0	(800) 645-6561
Fidelity Ginnie Mae Portfolio	1,000	0	(800) 544-6666
Lexington GNMA Income Fund	1,000	0	(800) 526-0056
T. Rowe Price GNMA Fund	1,000	0	(800) 638-5660
Vanguard Fixed Income—GNMA	3,000	0	(800) 662-2739

INDEX

Accrued interest, 33–34

Banks
  and commission, 12–13
Basis points, 29–30
Bills. *see* Treasury bills
Bearer securities, 39
Bonds. *see* Treasury bonds
Borrowing, 41–42
Brokers
  and commission, 12–13
  discount, 14
Bureau of the Public Debt, 15

Callability, 35–36
CATS. *see* Certificate of Accrual on
  Treasury Securities
CD. *see* Certificate of deposit
Certificate of Accrual on Treasury
  Securities (CATS), 53
Certificate of deposit (CD), 9–10
Commission, 12
  on Treasury notes and bonds,
    17–18

Debt securities, 5

Fannie Mae. *see* Federal National
  Mortgage Association
FDIC. *see* Federal Deposit
  Insurance Corporation
Federal Deposit Insurance
  Corporation (FDIC), 8–9
Federal Home Loan Banks, 7
Federal National Mortgage
  Association (FNMA), 48
  tax advantages, 48
Federal Reserve Banks, 82–85
Federal Savings and Loan
  Insurance Corporation (FSLIC),
  8–9
Flower bonds, 59–60
FNMA. *see* Federal National
  Mortgage Association
Forms
  1040, 33, 44
  1040A, 44
  W-9, 15
FSLIC. *see* Federal Savings and
  Loan Insurance Corporation

Ginnie Mae. *see* Government
  National Mortgage Association
GNMA. *see* Government National
  Mortgage Association
Government agencies, 7
Government deficit, 3–4
Government lending, 1–10
Government National Mortgage
  Association (Ginnie Mae;
  GNMA), 7, 43, 47–50
  certificates, 48–49
  tax advantages, 48
  taxes, 50
  trusts and mutual funds, 49–50
Government securities
  advantages, 1–2, 8–10
  attraction, 4
  liquidity, 2, 6–7
  maturity, 6
  safety, 1–2
  types, 5–7
  variety, 6

Inflation, 68
Interest, 32–34
  accrued, 33–34
  and basis points, 29–30
  Treasury bill calculation, 32
  on Treasury bonds, 17, 32–33
  on Treasury notes, 17, 32–33
Interest rates, 3–4
  attraction to
    government securities, 4
  fluctuation, 3–4
Internal Revenue Service (IRS),
  15, 52
Investment
  growth versus income, 68–69
  and inflation, 68, 70–71
  objectives, 67–69
  and Treasury bills, 70–71
IRA, 52
IRS. *see* Internal Revenue Service

Keogh, 52

Liquidity, 6–7, 9–10
  definition, 2

Margin accounts, 41–42

About the Authors

ARNOLD CORRIGAN, noted financial expert, is the author of *How Your IRA Can Make You a Millionaire* and is a frequent guest on financial talk shows. A senior officer of a large New York investment advisory firm, he holds Bachelor's and Master's degrees in economics from Harvard and has written for *Barron's* and other financial publications.

PHYLLIS C. KAUFMAN, the originator of the *No Nonsense Guides*, is a Philadelphia attorney and theatrical producer. A graduate of Brandeis University, she was an editor of the law review at Temple University School of Law. She is listed in *Who's Who in American Law*, *Who's Who of American Women*, *Who's Who in Finance and Industry*, and *Foremost Women of the Twentieth Century*.